Microsoft Exchange Server PowerShell Essentials

Leverage the power of basic Windows PowerShell scripts to manage your Exchange messaging environment

Biswanath Banerjee

[PACKT] enterprise
PUBLISHING
professional expertise distilled

BIRMINGHAM - MUMBAI

Microsoft Exchange Server PowerShell Essentials

First published: February 2016

Production reference: 1190216

Published by Packt Publishing Ltd.
Livery Place
35 Livery Street
Birmingham B3 2PB, UK.

ISBN 978-1-78217-603-9

www.packtpub.com

Credits

Author
Biswanath Banerjee

Reviewer
Mark Andrews

Commissioning Editor
Taron Pereira

Acquisition Editor
Manish Nainani

Content Development Editor
Kajal Thapar

Technical Editor
Gebin George

Copy Editor
Yesha Gangani

Project Coordinator
Dinesh Rathe

Proofreader
Safis Editing

Indexer
Rekha Nair

Production Coordinator
Melwyn Dsa

Cover Work
Melwyn Dsa

About the Author

Biswanath Banerjee has been working with Exchange Servers since 2005 in various roles in support, training, and consulting. Spanning an IT career of over 14 years, he has worked on multiple Active Directory and Exchange migration projects. He specializes in Planning and Deployment of Microsoft Infrastructure Solutions such as Active Directory, Exchange, Lync, Skype for Business, and various Office 365 services.

About the Reviewer

Mark Andrews career in technology has been a varied one. Over the last 18 years, he has held several different positions ranging from customer service to quality assurance. Throughout all of these positions, the responsibility of configuration management and build management has always fallen either to Mark personally or to one of the groups that he managed; because of his "keeping a hand in" management style, he has been involved closely with the scripting and automation framework for this area. Creating scripted frameworks that intercommunicate across machine/operating system/domain boundaries is a passion for him.

www.PacktPub.com

eBooks, discount offers, and more

Did you know that Packt offers eBook versions of every book published, with PDF and ePub files available? You can upgrade to the eBook version at www.PacktPub.com and as a print book customer, you are entitled to a discount on the eBook copy. Get in touch with us at customercare@packtpub.com for more details.

At www.PacktPub.com, you can also read a collection of free technical articles, sign up for a range of free newsletters and receive exclusive discounts and offers on Packt books and eBooks.

https://www2.packtpub.com/books/subscription/packtlib

Do you need instant solutions to your IT questions? PacktLib is Packt's online digital book library. Here, you can search, access, and read Packt's entire library of books.

Why subscribe?

- Fully searchable across every book published by Packt
- Copy and paste, print, and bookmark content
- On demand and accessible via a web browser

Instant updates on new Packt books

Get notified! Find out when new books are published by following @PacktEnterprise on Twitter or the *Packt Enterprise* Facebook page.

Table of Contents

Preface

PowerShell has become one of the most important skills in an Exchange administrator's armory. PowerShell has proved its mettle so widely that, if you're not already starting to learn PowerShell, then you're falling behind the industry. It isn't difficult to learn PowerShell at all. In fact, if you've ever run commands from a CMD prompt, then you'll be able to start using PowerShell straight away.

This book will walk you through the essentials of PowerShell in Microsoft Exchange Server, and make sure you understand its nitty gritty effectively. There are a lot of examples and scripts that will demonstrate how you can use PowerShell to be more effective and save time as an administrator, which otherwise would have been spent performing repetitive tasks.

Microsoft Exchange PowerShell Essentials will provide all the required details for Active Directory, System, and Exchange administrators to help them understand Windows PowerShell and build the required scripts to manage the Exchange Infrastructure.

What this book covers

Chapter 1, *Getting Started with PowerShell*, provides an introduction to Windows PowerShell, which will build a strong foundation for the latter chapters.

Chapter 2, *Learning Recipient Management*, teaches you ways to manage recipients in an Exchange organization.

Chapter 3, *Handling Distribution Groups*, is about managing different distribution groups as it plays a major role in the Exchange Administration.

Chapter 4, *Exchange Security*, talks about securing Exchange and delegating access to administration tasks using Role-Based Access Control.

Chapter 5, Everything about Microsoft Exchange Policies, covers how to manage address books, email addresses, and Retention Policies in Exchange 2013 and Exchange 2016.

Chapter 6, Handling Exchange Server Roles, talks about configuring Exchange Client Access such as POP, IMAP, Outlook Anywhere, ActiveSync, and different Transport Services.

Chapter 7, Auditing and E-Discovery, reviews auditing and discovery features in Exchange that will help Organizations meet their Compliance and e-discovery requirements.

Chapter 8, Managing High Availability, uses our knowledge of PowerShell to manage high availability for Exchange 2013 and 2016 Organization.

Chapter 9, Exploring EWS Managed API, reviews Exchange Web Services application programming interface (API) and its usage in managing an Exchange On Premise and Online Organization.

Chapter 10, Common Administration Tasks, reviews some of the common administrative tasks in Exchange and uses PowerShell to save time and effort spent in performing repetitive jobs.

What you need for this book

The following is a list of softwares and supported operating systems required for this book:

- Software required Exchange Server 2013 or 2016
- OS required — Windows 2008 R2, Windows 2012, or Windows 2012 R2
- Hardware Required:

Component	Requirement
Processor	• x64 architecture-based computer with Intel processor that supports Intel 64 architecture (formerly known as Intel EM64T) • AMD processor that supports the AMD64 platform • Intel Itanium IA64 processors not supported
Memory	Varies depending on Exchange roles that are installed: • **Mailbox** 8GB minimum • **Edge Transport** 4GB minimum

Component	Requirement
Paging file size	The minimum of page file size must be set to physical RAM plus 10 MB, to a maximum size of 32778 MB if you're using more than 32GB of RAM.
Disk space	• At least 30 GB on the drive on which you install Exchange • An additional 500 MB of available disk space for each Unified Messaging (UM) language pack that you plan to install • 200 MB of available disk space on the system drive • A hard disk that stores the message queue database on with at least 500 MB of free space
Drive	DVD-ROM drive, local, or network accessible
Screen resolution	1024 x 768 pixels or higher

To view complete system requirements of Exchange Server 2016, you can log on to `https://technet.microsoft.com/en-us/library/aa996719(v=exchg.160).aspx`.

Who this book is for

This book is for administrators with a basic or limited understanding of Windows PowerShell and who want to increase their skill set in managing both the Exchange On Premise and Online environments.

Conventions

In this book, you will find a number of text styles that distinguish between different kinds of information. Here are some examples of these styles and an explanation of their meaning.

Code words in text, database table names, folder names, filenames, file extensions, pathnames, dummy URLs, user input, and Twitter handles are shown as follows: "In MS-DOS and Windows 9X, the shell was `command.com`, and it was `cmd.exe` for Windows NT family of the operating system."

A block of code is set as follows:

```
$x = 12
$ = 34
```

When we wish to draw your attention to a particular part of a code block, the relevant lines or items are set in bold:

```
[default]
exten => s,1,Dial(Zap/1|30)
exten => s,2,Voicemail(u100)
exten => s,102,Voicemail(b100)
exten => i,1,Voicemail(s0)
```

Any command-line input or output is written as follows:

```
PS C:\> Set-ExecutionPolicy RemoteSigned
```

New terms and **important words** are shown in bold. Words that you see on the screen, for example, in menus or dialog boxes, appear in the text like this: " You can review the settings through Exchange Admin Center (EAC) by navigating to the **Mail Flow | email address** "

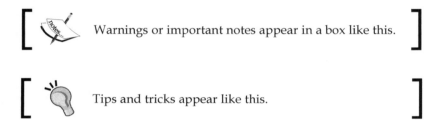

Warnings or important notes appear in a box like this.

Tips and tricks appear like this.

Reader feedback

Feedback from our readers is always welcome. Let us know what you think about this book—what you liked or disliked. Reader feedback is important for us as it helps us develop titles that you will really get the most out of.

To send us general feedback, simply e-mail feedback@packtpub.com, and mention the book's title in the subject of your message.

If there is a topic that you have expertise in and you are interested in either writing or contributing to a book, see our author guide at www.packtpub.com/authors.

Customer support

Now that you are the proud owner of a Packt book, we have a number of things to help you to get the most from your purchase.

Downloading the example code

You can download the example code files for this book from your account at http://www.packtpub.com. If you purchased this book elsewhere, you can visit http://www.packtpub.com/support and register to have the files e-mailed directly to you.

You can download the code files by following these steps:

1. Log in or register to our website using your e-mail address and password.
2. Hover the mouse pointer on the **SUPPORT** tab at the top.
3. Click on **Code Downloads & Errata**.
4. Enter the name of the book in the **Search** box.
5. Select the book for which you're looking to download the code files.
6. Choose from the drop-down menu where you purchased this book from.
7. Click on **Code Download**.

Once the file is downloaded, please make sure that you unzip or extract the folder using the latest version of:

- WinRAR / 7-Zip for Windows
- Zipeg / iZip / UnRarX for Mac
- 7-Zip / PeaZip for Linux

Downloading the color images of this book

We also provide you with a PDF file that has color images of the screenshots/diagrams used in this book. The color images will help you better understand the changes in the output. You can download this file from https://www.packtpub.com/sites/default/files/downloads/MicrosoftExchangeServerPowerShellEssentials_ColoredImages.pdf.

Errata

Although we have taken every care to ensure the accuracy of our content, mistakes do happen. If you find a mistake in one of our books—maybe a mistake in the text or the code—we would be grateful if you could report this to us. By doing so, you can save other readers from frustration and help us improve subsequent versions of this book. If you find any errata, please report them by visiting http://www.packtpub.com/submit-errata, selecting your book, clicking on the **Errata Submission Form** link, and entering the details of your errata. Once your errata are verified, your submission will be accepted and the errata will be uploaded to our website or added to any list of existing errata under the Errata section of that title.

To view the previously submitted errata, go to https://www.packtpub.com/books/content/support and enter the name of the book in the search field. The required information will appear under the **Errata** section.

Piracy

Piracy of copyrighted material on the Internet is an ongoing problem across all media. At Packt, we take the protection of our copyright and licenses very seriously. If you come across any illegal copies of our works in any form on the Internet, please provide us with the location address or website name immediately so that we can pursue a remedy.

Please contact us at copyright@packtpub.com with a link to the suspected pirated material.

We appreciate your help in protecting our authors and our ability to bring you valuable content.

Questions

If you have a problem with any aspect of this book, you can contact us at questions@packtpub.com, and we will do our best to address the problem.

1
Getting Started with PowerShell

This chapter will provide introduction to Windows PowerShell that is required for the rest of the chapters of this book. You will learn about the usage of Windows PowerShell cmdlets, variables, arrays, and loops. You will also learn the use of the PowerShell Help system. We will cover the concept of filtering and exporting objects using pipelines and the usage of loops and conditional statements. This chapter will create a foundation, and we will use subsequent chapters to build this foundation.

The following topics will be discussed in this chapter:

- Introducing Windows PowerShell
- Understanding PowerShell syntax
- Understanding the help system
- Understanding logging and transcripts
- Using variables
- Using pipelines
- Using looping
- Using arrays
- Using filters and exporting data
- Using If statements
- Writing a basic script

Introducing Windows PowerShell

Windows PowerShell is the evolution of the Windows command-line shell, which provides a scripting environment for MS-DOS and the Windows operating system. In MS-DOS and Windows 9X, the shell was `command.com`, and it was `cmd.exe` for Windows NT family of the operating system. In the UNIX world, there are different shells such as SH, KSH, CSH, and BASH.

Almost all of these shells provide an environment to execute a command or utility and present the output as text. These shells have some built-in commands such as `dir` in `cmd.exe` in Windows NT or later versions, but these built-in commands are limited; and hence, new utilities are written to fill the gap. Shells supported the use of a scripting language (batch files) to automate tasks. There were limitations when it came to creating complex scripts and automating all other aspects provided by a **Graphical User Interface (GUI)** as equivalent commands are not exposed and the scripting language was basic.

Windows scripting host (`Wscript.exe`) and its command-line counterpart called `Cscript.exe` was introduced in 1998 with the release of Windows 98 to address some of the challenges. It is a language-independent scripting environment and allows scripts written in Jscript and VBScript using the APIs exposed by applications. There were deficiencies in this scripting environment due to limited documentation and interoperability issues with shell and security vulnerabilities. There were several security breaches as computer viruses exploited features provided by WSH. There were a few other attempts made by Microsoft to build utilities for specific purpose — for example, netsh — with their list of supported command sets, but they were not integrated with the shell and were inoperable.

In 2005, Microsoft released a new shell called Monad (also known as **Microsoft Shell(MSH)**), which is designed to automate a wide range of administrative tasks and is based on a new design as opposed to its predecessors.

Similar to the `command.com` and `cmd.exe` shells, Windows PowerShell can run three types of programs: built-in commands, external programs, and scripts. However, unlike a command shell, the built-in commands are not embedded into the shell environment but are available as modules in one or more `.DLL` files. This allows both Microsoft and vendors to write custom modules to manage their applications using PowerShell. Now, most of Microsoft and vendor's applications support management through Windows PowerShell, for example, Windows Server, Exchange Server, SharePoint, Lync Server/Skype for business, and VMWare.

Windows PowerShell is different than its predecessors in the following ways:

- Windows PowerShell processes objects instead of text that are based on the .Net framework and provide lots of built-in commands

- All commands use the same command parser instead of different parser for each utility, which makes the use of PowerShell consistent and easier as compared to the earlier shell environments

- Administrators can still use the tools and utilities that they are used to in Windows PowerShell such as Net, SC, and `Reg.exe`

- As PowerShell is based on the .NET framework, one can write their own cmdlets using Microsoft Visual Studio and languages supported by the **Common Language Runtime (CLR)** such as C#

With the release of PowerShell 2.0, some APIs (application programming interface) were released that could be used to invoke PowerShell commands right from within your applications. Applications can then use certain PowerShell commands to perform a specific operation, which earlier could only be performed by GUI.

Starting from Exchange Server 2007, this capability has been used to its best advantage as will be explained over the course of the book. Learning PowerShell will help you in managing Microsoft, vendor applications, and services that support PowerShell. It will provide you the skillset required to manage and automate different aspects of Microsoft cloud-based offerings such as Office 365 and Windows Azure. Both of these support PowerShell and have specific modules for management. However, our focus in this book will be on managing Exchange through Windows PowerShell. At times, GUI is strictly used for illustration.

If you are interested in a .Net development, you can write your own cmdlet (pronounced as `command-lets`) in PowerShell that will perform a specific operation. For this, you will need PowerShell 2.0 **Software Development Kit (SDK)** and Visual Studio Express Edition. Both of these are free downloads.

You can download the example code files for this book from your account at `http://www.packtpub.com`. If you purchased this book elsewhere, you can visit `http://www.packtpub.com/support` and register to have the files e-mailed directly to you.

The following table summarizes the history of the different versions of Windows PowerShell:

Version	Year released	Operating systems	Features
1	2006	Windows Server 2003, Windows Server 2008, Windows XP SP2, and Windows Vista	First release
2	2009	Windows XP SP3, Windows Server 2003 SP2, Windows Vista SP1, Windows Server 2008 R2, and Windows 7	Remoting, Eventing, jobs, modules, ISE, and Exception handling
3	2012	Windows Server 2012 and Windows 8	Session connectivity, Scheduled jobs, update-help, and resumable sessions
4	2013	Windows Server 2012 R2, Windows 8.1, Windows 7 SP1, Windows Server 2008 R2 SP1, and Windows Server 2012	Desired State Configuration, Enhanced debugging, exportable help, and network diagnostics
5.0	2015	In Public Preview at the time of writing this book	OneGet, PowerShellGet, class definitions, and switch management improvements

Understanding PowerShell syntax

Windows PowerShell uses a verb-noun pair as a naming system. The name of each cmdlet includes a standard verb hyphenated with a specific noun. Verbs are used for specific actions in Windows PowerShell, and nouns are used to describe objects by users and system administrators. Here are some of the examples that show how little effort is required to work with cmdlets, and one does not have to memorize them.

Nouns in a cmdlet describe what the cmdlet will act on. For example, get-process, get-service, stop-process and stop-service. If this is used regularly, one can get to know the standard set of verbs and nouns used in PowerShell. With these verb-noun pair, hundreds of cmdlet names can be remembered and used.

You will be able to recognize the operation performed by a cmdlet by just reading the name as it is mostly apparent about the name used by a new command should relate to the operation. For example, get-computer will give you a list of computers on your network. Get-date and get-time will display the system date and time respectively. Similarly, stop-computer will shut down a computer. Set-date and set-time will set the system's date and time.

Let's look at how to list all the commands that have the particular verbs called Get and Set using Get-command with the -verb parameter. The output of this command is piped to display in a table format (more on this will be covered later in the *Usage of pipelines* section).

```
PS C:\> Get-Command -Verb get | Format-Table

CommandType       Name                               ModuleName
-----------       ----                               ----------
Alias             Get-GPPermissions                  GroupPolicy
Alias             Get-ProvisionedAppxPackage         Dism
Function          Get-AppxLastError                  Appx
Function          Get-AppxLog                        Appx
Function          Get-BCClientConfiguration          BranchCache
Function          Get-BCContentServerConfiguration   BranchCache
Function          Get-BCDataCache                    BranchCache
Function          Get-BCDataCacheExtension           BranchCache
```

In the next example, we will just use instead of a format table:

```
PS C:\> Get-Command -Verb set | ft

CommandType       Name                        ModuleName
-----------       ----                        ----------
Alias             Set-GPPermissions           GroupPolicy
Function          Set-BCAuthentication        BranchCache
Function          Set-BCCache                 BranchCache
Function          Set-BCDataCacheEntryMaxAge  BranchCache
Function          Set-BCMinSMBLatency         BranchCache
Function          Set-BCSecretKey             BranchCache
Function          Set-ClusteredScheduledTask  ScheduledTasks
```

Now, let's use the -Noun parameter, and we will find a list of commands that affect the same object type. For example, if you want to see commands that are available for managing computers, type the following command:

```
PS C:\> Get-Command -Noun computer | ft

CommandType       Name                  ModuleName
-----------       ----                  ----------
Cmdlet            Add-Computer          Microsoft.PowerShell.Management
Cmdlet            Checkpoint-Computer   Microsoft.PowerShell.Management
Cmdlet            Remove-Computer       Microsoft.PowerShell.Management
Cmdlet            Rename-Computer       Microsoft.PowerShell.Management
Cmdlet            Restart-Computer      Microsoft.PowerShell.Management
Cmdlet            Restore-Computer      Microsoft.PowerShell.Management
Cmdlet            Stop-Computer         Microsoft.PowerShell.Management
```

Traditionally, the commands in the earlier shells usually do not have a consistent parameter name. Sometimes, they don't have a name at all, and even if they do, they are abbreviated to make typing easier. But, this makes it difficult for new users to understand the parameters that are used. In Windows PowerShell, consistency is encouraged by using developer guidance on the usage of parameter names.

The names of the parameters in Windows PowerShell have a hyphen '-' prepended to them to allow PowerShell to demarcate them as parameters. In the get-command -Noun example, the name of the parameter is Noun and is typed as -Noun.

The cmdlets in Windows PowerShell support several common parameters as the PowerShell engine controls these parameters. So, no matter how they are implemented, they will behave in a similar way. Another way to drive the consistency and learning of Windows PowerShell are some of the common parameters like — Confirm, WhatIf, outvariable, warningaction, warningvariable, debug, and verbose.

Understanding the help system

This section will cover the use of help in Windows PowerShell. The help topic for a particular command or conceptual help can assist an administrator who is new to Windows PowerShell or using a particular set of cmdlets to understand its syntax and usage.

The Help parameter (?)

The -? parameter with a cmdlet will display Windows PowerShell help for the cmdlet:

```
PS C:\> get-process -?

NAME
    Get-Process

SYNOPSIS
    Gets the processes that are running on the local computer or a remote computer.

SYNTAX
    Get-Process [[-Name] <String[]>] [-ComputerName <String[]>] [-FileVersionInfo] [-Module] [<CommonParameters>]

    Get-Process [-ComputerName <String[]>] [-FileVersionInfo] [-Module] -InputObject <Process[]> [<CommonParameters>]

    Get-Process [-ComputerName <String[]>] [-FileVersionInfo] [-Module] -Id <Int32[]> [<CommonParameters>]

    Get-Process -Id <Int32[]> -IncludeUserName [<CommonParameters>]

    Get-Process -IncludeUserName -InputObject <Process[]> [<CommonParameters>]

    Get-Process [[-Name] <String[]>] -IncludeUserName [<CommonParameters>]
```

The Get-Help cmdlet

The `Get-Help` cmdlet displays help information about PowerShell cmdlets. Some of the examples are discussed as follows.

The following example gives you the help files from the PowerShell help system one page at a time:

```
PS C:\>get-help * | more
```

If you know the alias of the cmdlet you are trying to get help for, use the `-detailed` parameter for full help:

```
PS C:\>get-help gps -detailed
```

If you are not sure of the exact parameter but remember the initial letter, use the following to get help:

```
PS C:\>get-help get-process -parameter i*
```

This lists all the parameters of the cmdlet `get-process`:

```
PS C:\>get-help get-process -Parameter *
```

This provides help with the syntax of the `select-object` cmdlet:

```
PS C:\>(get-help select-object).syntax
```

There are other properties of the help object such as input types, module name, examples, and more. If you are looking to find all the properties and methods of help object type called `get-help <cmdlet-name> | get-member`, for example, `PS C:\> get-help get-Service | get-member`.

Understanding Logging and Transcripts

The transcript feature in PowerShell helps you to record all your cmdlets and activities at the prompt. This feature is not available for use in the PowerShell application during the writing of this book. This will help you capture all the commands and outputs from the commands that appear in the console in a text file that you specify using the `start-transcript` cmdlet.

The `Start-transcript` cmdlet initializes a transcript file, and then creates records of all the subsequent actions in the PowerShell session.

The syntax is shown as follows:

```
Start-Transcript [[-Path] <String>] [-Append] [-Force] [-NoClobber] [-Confirm] [-WhatIf] [<CommonParameters>]
Start-Transcript [[-LiteralPath] <String>] [-Append] [-Force] [-NoClobber] [-Confirm] [-WhatIf] [<CommonParameters>]
```

Here are some of the important parameters that you should know about the `start-transcript` cmdlet. To save the transcript file to a specified path, use the `-Path` parameter. You cannot use wildcards when you set the path, but you can also use variables. The directories in the path must exist or the command will fail.

The default behavior of the `Start-Transcript` cmdlet is to overwrite any file that is in the transcript path unless the `-noClobber` parameter is specified, which prevents Windows PowerShell from overwriting an existing file.

The `-Append` parameter will add the new transcript to the end of an existing file. For example, take a look at the following:

```
PS C:\> Start-Transcript -Path C:\transcript\transcript01.txt -NoClobber
```

When you want to stop recording the transcript, you can either exit the console or type `Stop-transcript`. The `Stop-Transcript` cmdlet requires no additional parameters.

The `Stop-transcript` cmdlet stops recording actions that was started by the `start-transcript` cmdlet. Use the following syntax:

```
PS C:\> stop-transcript
```

Using variables

In PowerShell, the data is stored, retrieved, and modified using the methods listed next. In this section, we are going to cover only variables:

- A variable is used to store bits of information
- Arrays are used to store information in an index
- A Hash table uses key-value pair to store data

A variable is virtual storage to store information that will be utilized later in a script or the information that is the output of running a script. Variables can contain different data types such as text strings, objects, and integers. There are few special variables that you can use, which are defined in PowerShell.

The examples of some of the special variables are as follows:

Special Variable	Description
$_	This is the same as the $PS item. It contains the current object in the pipeline object and can be used in commands that perform an action on all or selected objects in a pipeline.
$Home	This contains the path of the user's' home directory, typically C:\Users\<UserName>.
$Error	This is an array that contains the errors in the current execution. The first element in the array ($Error[0]) will contain the most recent error.
$NULL	This is an automatic variable that contains a NULL or empty value.

If you are looking for a full list of automatic variables available for use in Windows PowerShell, type the following:

```
PS C:\> get-help about_automatic_variables
```

In PowerShell, all the variable names must start with the $ character. Data is assigned to a variable using the = operator:

```
PS C:\> $Number = 25
```

There are the Set-Variable and Get-Variable cmdlets that can also be used to set and retrieve the values of the variable.

Here, the value 401B is passed to the variable ExamCode:

```
PS C:\> Set-Variable -Name ExamCode -Value 401B
PS C:\> Get-Variable ExamCode
```

A little bit about operators that are used for assignment and comparison of values assigned to variables.

Assignment operators

The following operators are used to assign values to variables and carry out numeric operations before the assignment:

Operator	Description
=	A specific value is assigned to a variable using the equal to = operator
+=	The variable value is increased by a specific number
-=	The variable value is decreased by the number specified

Operator	Description
*=	This operator is used to multiply the value stored in a variable by a specified number
/=	This divides the value by a specific number
%=	In this case, the value stored in the variable is divided by the specified number and the modulus (remainder) is stored in the variable
++	This increases the value of variables by 1
--	This decreases the value of variables by 1

The example assigns the value of to the variable called $Book:

$Bookk = "Microsoft Exchange PowerShell Essentials"

In the previous example, the $Book variable is created as we have assigned the value to the variable using the assignment operator. If you look at the following example, the first statement creates a $x variable and assigns a value of 12. The second statement has changed its value to 34:

```
$x = 12
$ = 34
```

While scripting, there is a need to combine operations such as addition, subtraction, and assignment to variables. For example, the following statements will produce the exact same output:

```
$i += 3
$i = ($i +3)
```

Similarly, if you want to multiply first and then assign, use any of the following statements:

```
$n *= 4
$n = ($n * 4)
```

If you want to use a specific data type, you have to override how PowerShell stores values in variables. This can be achieved by strongly typed variables or casting them. For example, the first one is a variable that will only store integers and the second one will store strings:

```
[int]$Number = 12
[string]$Book = "Microsoft Exchange PowerShell Essentials"
```

Now, let's take a look at an example of what happens if we do not specify the correct datatype to a variable. Here, we have stored the value of 56 in the $x variable as a string. The next statement adds the value of 8 to the variable. The output will be displayed as a string and numeric operation will be performed. As a best practice, you should always cast your variables with the correct data type:

```
[string]$s =  56
$s += 8
$s
568
```

You will not be able to recast a variable without changing its value. In our previous example, we have casted $Book as a string value and stored the value of *Microsoft Exchange PowerShell Essentials* in it. If you try to use the following statement, you will get an error message, which essentially means that you have to change the value before you cast the variable to a different data type:

```
[int]$Book
```

Cannot convert value string to type System.Int32. Error—"Input string was not in a correct format."

```
At line:1 char:1
+ [int]$b
+ ~~~~~~~
    + CategoryInfo          : InvalidArgument: (:) [],
RuntimeException
    + FullyQualifiedErrorId : InvalidCastFromStringToInteger
```

Now, let's use the Windows PowerShell help system to learn more about other assignment operators:

```
PS C:\> get-help about_assignment_operators
```

Comparison operators

These operators are used to compare values and match specific patterns. Here is the list of comparison operators available, and these operators are case insensitive. If you want to make these operators case sensitive or insensitive, precede c or i in front of the following operator:

- eq
- -ne
- -gt
- -ge

- `-lt`
- `-le`
- `-Like`
- `-NotLike`
- `-Match`
- `-NotMatch`
- `-Contains`
- `-NotContains`
- `-In`
- `-NotIn`
- `-Replace`

Take a look at the following examples:

`-eq` — Equal to:

```
PS C:\> "apple" -eq "apple"
True
PS C:\> "apple" -eq "orange"
False
```

`-ne` — Not Equal to:

```
PS C:\> "apple" -ne "apple"
False
PS C:\> "apple" -ne "orange"
True
```

`-gt` — Greater than:

```
PS C:\> 5 -gt 8
False
PS C:\> 23,34,56 -gt 50
56
```

`Like` — Match using the wildcard character (*).

Take a look at the following examples:

```
PS C:\> "Windows PowerShell" -like "*shell"
True
PS C:\> "Windows PowerShell", "Server" -like "*shell"
        Windows PowerShell
```

Review the help for other comparison operators:

```
PS C:\> get-help about_comparison_operators
```

Using pipelines

A pipeline is a series of cmdlet statements connected through the pipeline (|) character (ASCII 124). Pipelines are used to send the output objects from one command as an input to another command. This can be used in scripts and console to build complex statements.

The output of Get-Service is piped to more command that displays information one screen at a time:

```
Get-Servince | more
```

You can use pipelines to build complex queries. For example, the following example will get the output of the Get-Service cmdlet and pipe it to the Where-Object cmdlet that will filter the services whose names match the MSExchange text, and the status is set to Running. The logical and operator is used in this case to combine the two conditions:

```
Get-Service | Where-Object {($_.Name -like "MSExchange*") -and ($_.Status
-eq "Running")}
```

So far, we saw how to take output from one command and feed it into the next one. Now, let's take it further by adding one more piping. The following statement will get the output of the Get-Service cmdlet and pass it to Where-object where it will filter it for Exchange services, which are stopped, and then it will pass the output using another pipeline to Start-Service cmdlet. So, using this one-line command, you can check which Exchange Services are not running and start them. We have used the—autosize parameter to format the output based on the number of columns and their sizes:

```
Get-Service | Where-Object {($_.Name -like "MSExchange*") -and ($_.Status
-eq "Stopped")} | Start-Service
```

Using loops

In this section, we will review the usage of loops in Windows PowerShell. Every scripting language has multiple ways to loop through an array of items and execute a block of statements. Windows PowerShell has a variety of looping mechanisms described next.

The Do loop

Here is another way to run a statement block based on a conditional result. The Do loop is used with While and Until keywords to run a script block along with a conditional statement. Both the loop Do-While and Do-Until run once before the condition is evaluated. The command block is executed in a Do-While loop as long as the condition is true, whereas a Do-Until loop runs until a condition evaluates to be true.

The syntax of Do-While and Do-Until is the same. The following shows the syntax of the Do-While statement:

```
do {<command block>} while (<condition>)
do {<command block>} until (<condition>)
```

Examples are as follows:

Count to 5—In the following example, the statement is to use an increment operator with a $a variable and increment the value by 1 (as listed earlier in the assignment operators section of this chapter), and the condition is evaluated to be true until the value of a is less than 5. Here is how we will use the loop in a single line in PowerShell:

```
PS C:\> Do { $a++ ; Write-Host $a } while($a -ne 5)
```

The previous statement can be used in a different way where a carriage return is used instead of a semi-colon:

```
PS C:\>   Do { $a++
            Write-Host $a
        } while($a -ne 5)
```

The Do-Until loop executes the statement list until the condition is false. Once the condition evaluates to be true, the loop exits.

In the following example, the script block will write the output of the variable to the console and increment it by 1, and the process is repeated until the condition, which is the value, becomes greater than 5 is evaluated to be false. Once $Count exceeds number 5, changing the condition to true, the loop exits:

```
PS C:\>   $Count = 1
do {Write-Host $Count; $Count++}
until ($Count -gt 5)
```

ForEach loops

The ForEach statement is used to iterate through a series of items in a collection. A typical collection is to traverse through the items in an array. You can specify within the ForEach loop a command or a command block against each item in the array:

Syntax is as follows:

```
                              foreach ($<Element> in $< group of items>)
{Command Block>}
```

The following ForEach loop displays the values of the $Number array.

In Windows PowerShell, the entire ForEach statement should be in one line for execution. Here is an example:

```
$Numbers = "1","2","3","4","5"; foreach ($No in $Numbers) {Write-Host $No}
```

If you are using a PowerShell script file, you can use the ForEach statement using multiple lines in a .ps1 file:

```
$Numbers = "1","2","3","4","5"
foreach ($No in $Numbers)
{
Write-Host $No
}
```

In the previous example, the $Numbers array is used to store values from 1 to 5. The ForEach statement loops through each of the items in the $Number array. In the first time, it sets the $No variable with value 1, second time with value 2, and so on. The loops exit when the value of 5 is reached.

We will use ForEach in the remaining chapters with cmdlets that return a collection. For example, we will use ForEach to iterate through each of the file/directory returned by Get-ChildItem in this case:

```
foreach ($item in Get-ChildItem)
        {
                Write-Host $item
        }
```

Loop through an array of strings:

```
$Fruit = @("Apple","Peach","Banana","Strawberry")
foreach ($fruit in $fruit) {
  "$fruit = " + $fruit.length
}
The following example displays all the numbers in the series except 2:
foreach ($num in 1,2,3,4,5) {
  if ($num -eq 2) { continue } ; $num
}
```

While loops

The `While` loop is used to execute statements in the command block as long as the condition is evaluated to be `true`.

Here is the syntax of a While loop:

```
while (<condition to be evaluated>) {<Command Block>}
```

In a `while` statement, the condition is evaluated to be either `true` or `false`. As long as the condition is `true`, the command block is executed, which can be a combination of more commands running through each iteration of the loop.

The following example lists numbers from 1 to 9 as the value of variable is $value is evaluated to be `true` until its value is equal to 9:

```
while ($value -ne 9)
{
$value++
Write-Host $value
}
```

You can write the same command in PowerShell in one line as follows:

```
while($value -ne 9){$value++; Write-Host $value}
```

Note that there is a semi-colon (`;`) that separates the two commands in the command block. The first one increments the value of $value by 1, and the second command writes the output of $value to the console.

Using arrays

An array is a variable that stores multiple items that are either of the same or different data type. An array can be created by assigning multiple values to a variable separated by a comma. The operator is used to assign values is the assignment operator (=). The following example creates an array that contains numbers 34, 56, 2, 23, and 8:

```
$Array = 34, 56, 2, 23, 8
```

A range operator (..) can also be used to create and initialize an array. The following example will create an array that will store the numbers from 1 to 5:

```
$Number = 1..5
```

This will store the values 1, 2, 3, 4, and 5 into the $Number.

If you do not specify the data type during creation, PowerShell creates an array of type:System.Object[]. You can use the GetType() method to display the type of array object created. For instance, the data type of the $Number array will be listed by:

```
$Number.GetType().
```

If you need an array that can have items of a particular data type, use the strongly typed array by preceding the array variable name with the data type such as the following example where $intarray contains 32-bit integer values:

```
[int32[]]$intarray = 1000, 2000, 3000, 4000
```

This will result in $intarray containing only integers as we have specified that no values other than int32 data type is allowed as value in this array.

In Windows Powershell, you can create arrays consisting of any supported data type in the Microsoft .Net framework.

Now, let's take an example of an array with multiple data types:

```
$mixedArray = 6,"Hello",4.5,"World"
```

The array subexpression operator is used to create an array with zero or more objects. Use the following syntax for the operator @(...):

```
$mixedArray = @(6,"Hello",4.5,"World")
```

Some other examples are as follows:

The following example creates an empty array:

```
$EmptyArray = @()
```

Create an array with a single element:

```
$Array = @("Hello World")
```

Create a multidimensional array:

```
$MultiDimArray = @(
            (4,5,6),
            (24,30,36)
    )
```

Retrieving values from an array

If you type the array name, it will display all the items in that array:

```
$Array
```

The array number index starts at 0, so the first element will be accessed by this:

```
$Array[0]
```

This is similar to displaying the fifth element in the $Array use:

```
$Array[4]
```

The last element of the array will be displayed by -1. So, the following example displays the last four items:

```
$Array[-4..-1]
```

We have used the range operator (..) here, which can also be used to display the elements from values 1 to 5 in the next example:

```
$Array[1..5]
```

The (+) operator combines the elements of the array. Use the following example to display the elements at index 0, 1, 3, and 5 to 8:

```
$Array[0,1,3+5..8]
```

The length property of the Count alias will display the number of items in an array:

```
$Array.Count
```

While, ForEach, and For looping statements are used to display items in an array:

```
Foreach ($item in $Array) {$item}
```

The following For statement loops through and displays every third item in the array:

```
For ($n = 0; $n -le ($Array.length -1); $n+=3) {$Array[$n]}
```

The `While` statement is used to list the items in an array until the defined condition becomes false. The following example displays the items until the index position is less than 6:

```
$i=0
while($i -lt 5) {$a[$i]; $i++}
```

Now, let's look at manipulating items in arrays. The replacement of an item in an array can be done by using the assignment (=) operator and the index of the present item to be replaced. The following example replaces the fourth element with the value of 23:

```
$Array[3] = 23
```

The `SetValue` method can also be used to replace the value of items in an array. The following example replaces the third value (index position 2) with a value of 34:

```
$Array.SetValue(34,2)
```

The elements are added to the array by the use of the += operator. The following example adds an element of 250 to the `$Array` array:

```
$Array +=250
```

The default array class in PowerShell does not provide an easy way to delete the elements of the array. Array elements can be copied over to another array and old arrays can be deleted though. In the following example, the `$x` array will consist of all the items from `$array` except the third and fifth items:

```
$x = $array[0,1,3 + 5..($array.length - 1)]
```

Multiple arrays can be combined in a single array by using a plus operator (+). The following example creates three arrays `$a`, `$b`, and `$c` and combines them to `$x`, which will now have all the elements of the three arrays:

```
$a = 2,4,6,8,10
$b = 1,3,5,7,9
$c = 11,12,13,14,15
$x= $a+$b+$c
```

Arrays can be deleted by assigning the value of `$null` to the array; for example, `$array = $null`.

For additional help on arrays, use the following cmdlet:

```
PS C:\> get-help about_arrays
```

Using filters and exporting data

In order to understand how powerful Windows PowerShell is, you need to look at the filtering capabilities it offers. With an understanding of objects and pipelining, you can retrieve the exact information you are looking for. The *Usage of Pipeline* section talks about how pipelines can be used to pass one or more objects, which are the output of one command, and feed them into another cmdlet. In Windows PowerShell, there are commands that will help you to refine and get the desired output. Some of these cmdlets that we will look in this section are `Where-Object`, `Sort-Object`, `Select-Object`, and `Select-String`.

The `Where-Object` cmdlet helps you to filter the output returned by other cmdlets. For example, the `Get-service` cmdlet without any parameter retrieves information about the services installed on the computer on which it is called:

```
PS C:\> get-service

Status     Name              DisplayName
------     ----              -----------
Stopped    adfssrv           Active Directory Federation Services
Running    ADWS              Active Directory Web Services
Stopped    AeLookupSvc       Application Experience
Stopped    ALG               Application Layer Gateway Service
Running    AppHostSvc        Application Host Helper Service
Stopped    AppIDSvc          Application Identity
Stopped    Appinfo           Application Information
Stopped    AppMgmt           Application Management
Stopped    AppReadiness      App Readiness
Stopped    AppXSvc           AppX Deployment Service (AppXSVC)
Stopped    AudioEndpointBu... Windows Audio Endpoint Builder
```

Now, let's filter the output of `Get-Service` to find the list of services that are stopped:

```
PS C:\> Get-Service | Where-Object {$_.status -eq "stopped"}

Status     Name              DisplayName
------     ----              -----------
Stopped    adfssrv           Active Directory Federation Services
Stopped    AeLookupSvc       Application Experience
Stopped    ALG               Application Layer Gateway Service
Stopped    AppIDSvc          Application Identity
Stopped    Appinfo           Application Information
Stopped    AppMgmt           Application Management
Stopped    AppReadiness      App Readiness
Stopped    AppXSvc           AppX Deployment Service (AppXSVC)
Stopped    AudioEndpointBu... Windows Audio Endpoint Builder
Stopped    Audiosrv          Windows Audio
Stopped    Browser           Computer Browser
```

Windows PowerShell supports the following logical operators that we are going to use in our next example of filtering the output of a `Get-Service` cmdlet:

Operator	Description
-and	This is `true` only when both statements are `true`
-or	This is `true` when either or both statements are `true`
-xor	This is `true` if one condition is `true` and the other one is `false`
-not	The statement followed by this operator is negated
!	This is the same as the –`not` operator

We will now find services that are running whose name starts with Windows using the –`and` operator:

```
PS C:\> get-service | Where-Object {($_.Status -eq "running") -and ($_.Name -like "Win*")}

Status    Name                DisplayName
------    ----                -----------
Running   WindowsAzureGue...  Windows Azure Guest Agent
Running   WindowsAzureTel...  Windows Azure Telemetry Service
Running   Winmgmt             Windows Management Instrumentation
Running   WinRM               Windows Remote Management (WS-Manag...
```

By default, Windows PowerShell will sort the output of commands using an alphabetical order. You can then use the `Sort-object` cmdlet to sort it using any way you like. For example, the following example will first sort the output of the `Get-Process` cmdlet by the Process ID and then the CPU time:

```
PS C:\> get-process | Sort-Object ID, CPU

Handles  NPM(K)    PM(K)      WS(K) VM(M)   CPU(s)     Id ProcessName
-------  ------    -----      ----- -----   ------     -- -----------
      0       0        0          4     0                 0 Idle
    767       0      116        280     3   113.59        4 System
     55       2      280       1048     4     0.13      268 smss
    161      15     1876       7444    43     0.13      332 vds
    219      13     1636       3980    47     0.73      372 csrss
     90       9     1260       3380    39     0.08      424 csrss
    399      33     7988      12028    55     0.66      428 svchost
     79       7      704       3488    20     0.08      432 wininit
    126       7     1156       5472    67     0.17      460 winlogon
    321      15     4092      10128    35     3.09      520 services
   1779     143    54988      61972  1187   349.22      528 lsass
    446      14     4448      10580    41     2.31      664 svchost
    394      18     2996       6504    25     5.00      704 svchost
    159      12     1452      29756    92     7.31      756 csrss
    172      14    12008      21292    84     0.08      796 dwm
```

At times, you might need to filter your results based on certain specific property names. This is where the `Select-Object` cmdlet comes in handy. It selects the stated properties of a single or group of objects. You can use `Select-Object` to select objects that are unique in a group of objects It supports parameters such as `First`, `Last`, `Skip`, and `Index`. You can select one or multiple object properties using the `-Property` parameter. Let's take an example of the output of the `Get-Process` cmdlet, and let's say you are troubleshooting a performance issue on a server and are only interested to know about the CPU time and process name properties. The output of the `Get-Process` cmdlet will be piped to `Select-Object` with the `-property` parameter set to the process name and CPU. The `Format-list` cmdlet will format the output displayed in the console:

```
PS C:\> Get-Process | Select-Object -Property Processname, CPU | format-
list
```

Now, let's use another parameter called `-Unique` of `Select-Object`. This will select a single member from a number or objects with same properties and values. In the following example, you will notice that the `-Unique` parameter is case sensitive and reports "c" and "C" as unique.

```
PS C:\> $Char = "a", "A", "B", "c", "C", "c", "b", "B"
PS C:\> $Char | Select-Object -Unique
a
A
B
c
C
b
```

Another useful filtering cmdlet is `Select-String`, used to select text patterns in strings and files. If you are familiar with UNIX shells, it is used as `Grep` or `Findstr` in Windows. It can display all the matches or stop after the first match depending on the usage of the cmdlet. You can search files of Unicode text using this command as well.

First, we will create a file using the redirection operator (>) to store the list of services running on a server to a text file:

```
PS C:\> Get-Service > service.txt
```

Now, we will find the text "Network" and "Windows" to get a list of all the services that have the word in it. We will then use the −notmatch parameter to list all the services except this word:

```
PS C:\> select-string -Path .\service.txt -Pattern network, windows
service.txt:14:Stopped   AudioEndpointBu...   Windows Audio Endpoint Builder
service.txt:15:Stopped   Audiosrv             Windows Audio
service.txt:39:Running   EventLog             Windows Event Log
service.txt:43:Running   FontCache            Windows Font Cache Service
service.txt:44:Stopped   FontCache3.0.0.0     Windows Presentation Foundation Fon..
service.txt:65:Running   MpsSvc               Windows Firewall
service.txt:68:Stopped   msiserver            Windows Installer
service.txt:69:Stopped   napagent             Network Access Protection Agent
service.txt:70:Stopped   NcaSvc               Network Connectivity Assistant
```

Note that the search performed here is a case insensitive search; you can use the −case sensitive parameter to make it case sensitive, which means you won't get any output if you use the parameter with the previous command as there are no matches found.

Using If statements

In this section, we will use the if conditional statement If to execute statements based on a specific condition test to be true. We can also use the If command to do tests on more than one condition or even if all the other conditions are evaluated to be false.

The following example shows the If statement syntax:

```
if (<Condition1>)
        {<Command Block 1>}
[elseif (<Condition2>)
        {<Command Block 2>}]
[else
        {<Command Block 3>}]
```

We will use the if command to check the status of the services running on the computer, and if the status is stopped, it will be displayed in red and the running services will be displayed in green. We will use a combination of pipeline, the foreach-object cmdlet, and the if statement.

```
PS C:\> get-service | foreach-object {if ($_.status -eq "stopped")
{write-host -foregroundcolor red $_.Displayname}` else {write-host
-foregroundcolor green $_.Displayname }}
```

Let's take a look at another example where you would like to find whether a particular folder is created. We will use a Test-Path cmdlet, which will return true if it finds the folder and false if it does not. As I am using the statement on my Active Directory domain controller, the folder is not present under Program Files, and this is what you will see in the output:

```
PS C:\> $ExchangeFolder = "C:\Program Files\Microsoft\Exchange Server"
PS C:\> $FolderPresent = Test-Path $ExchangeFolder
PS C:\> if ($FolderPresent -eq $True) {Write-Host "Exchange installation
Folder found on this Server"} else {Write-Host "Exchange installation
folder not present"}
Exchange installation folder not present
```

Switch statements

A Switch statement is used to check multiple conditions. It is equivalent to a series of If statements. The Switch statement lists each condition and an optional action. If a condition is true, the action is performed:

Syntax:

```
Switch (<test-value>)
{
    <condition> {<action>}
    <condition> {<action>}
}
```

The Switch statement compares the value of 2 to each of the conditions listed. Once the test value matches the condition, the action is performed:

```
PS> switch (2)
 {
    1 {"It is one."}
    2 {"It is two."}
    3 {"It is three."}
    4 {"It is four."}
 }
It is two.
```

In the previous example, the value is compared to each condition in the list and there is a match for the value of 2. Let's take a look at the same example where we have added another condition that matches the value of 2:

```
PS> switch (2)
 {
    1 {"It is one."}
```

```
      2 {"It is two."}
      3 {"It is three."}
      4 {"It is four."}
      2 {"Two again."}
  }
It is two.
Two again.
```

Using the Break statement, you can directly switch to stop the comparison after a match and terminate the switch statement:

```
PS> switch (2)
  {
      1 {"It is one."}
      2 {"It is two."; Break}
      3 {"It is three."}
      4 {"It is four."}
      2 {"Two again."}
  }
It is two.
```

Writing a basic script

Now that we have covered the basics of Windows PowerShell, let's write our first script. PowerShell uses the .ps1 format to save scripts. Before we get into executing scripts, let's first understand the following PowerShell Script Execution Policies that are in place to prevent unwanted scripts from being executed on your computer.

The cmdlet Set-Execution Policy helps you to change the Policy of which scripts you can run on your computer. There are four different execution policies:

- **Restricted**: In this mode, you cannot run any script and can use Windows PowerShell to run cmdlets in the interactive mode only.

- **AllSigned**: Locally created and those signed by a trusted publisher can be run

- **RemoteSigned**: Scripts downloaded from another computer can run only if these are signed by a trusted publisher

- **Unrestricted**: All the scripts will run regardless of whether they are signed or not

Now, let's set the execution Policy to Remote Signed and verify using **Get-Execution** Policy cmdlet:

```
PS C:\> Set-ExecutionPolicy RemoteSigned
PS C:\> Get-ExecutionPolicy
```

I am going to introduce the PowerShell **Integrated Scripting Engine** (ISE) that makes it easier to run scripts with features, such as syntax-coloring, tab completion, IntelliSense, visual debugging, and context sensitive Help, as compared to the PowerShell console.

The following script will query the win32_logical disk WMI class. This is a representation of a local storage device on a Windows Computer. There are six possible Drive Types, and we will use a Switch statement to get the output in text describing the type of storage:

Summary

In this chapter, you learned the usage of the cmdlet syntax in Windows PowerShell and the help system. We also covered variables and arrays used to store data. This data can then be exported and filtered in a lot of different ways by the use of operators, pipelines, and loops. Finally, the use of If statement is reviewed, which can be used to run a block of code based on a conditional test. These basics will be used throughout the rest of this book in examples and scripts.

In the next chapter, we are going to look at ways to manage recipients in an Exchange organization.

2
Learning Recipient Management

Prior to the release of Exchange Server 2007, recipient management tasks were performed using Active Directory Users and computers, and there was no easy way to do bulk management and automation and scripting support was limited.

The release of Exchange Server 2007 introduced the Exchange management shell as a management tool, which was built at the top of Windows PowerShell. There was also a **Graphical User Interface (GUI)** tool called the Exchange management console. The later versions of Exchange such as Exchange 2010, Exchange 2013 and 2016 are built on this foundation. All the management tasks in starting Exchange 2007 and later can be performed using the Exchange management shell where a subset of management tasks can be performed by its GUI counterpart. The **Exchange management console (EMC)**, which was released with Exchange 2007 and 2010, has been deprecated and an HTML-based GUI tool called Exchange Admin Center (EAC) has been introduced in Exchange 2013/2016 due to some known issues with **Microsoft Management Console (MMC)** based tool in the earlier releases.

In this chapter, we will cover the following topics:

- Managing users
- Managing folder/calendar permissions
- Managing permissions
- Managing room mailboxes
- Import and export of objects
- Connecting from remote computers
- Mailbox reporting
- Automation with scripting agents
- Writing a basic script

Managing users

Let's take a look at the most common recipient type in an Exchange organization—
Mailbox enabled users. A mailbox in Exchange is associated with an Active Directory
user account. The mailbox provides users the capability to store messages, tasks,
notes, attachments and send and receive messages.

In this topic, we will cover how to manage mailbox enabled users, and we are going
to use the Exchange management shell to perform all the management activities.

Before proceeding further, let's review the permission model briefly here to
understand what permissions are required to perform user management tasks.
This will be covered in detail in *Chapter 4, Exchange Security*.

With the release of Exchange 2010 and later, Microsoft introduced **Role Based Access
Control (RBAC)**, which is a permission model to manage various aspects of an
Exchange organization. You do not need to rely on Active Directory **Access Control
Lists (ACLs)** as you did in the previous versions of Exchange such as Exchange 2007
and earlier. Microsoft tried to fix issues by modifying ACLs and their unintended
results such as carrying these modifications through upgrades and troubleshooting
permission issues to improve the delegation model in the Exchange management.

With RBAC, administrators and helpdesk staff now have a way to provide granular
access based on the task that a group is about to perform. I would like to stop here
and pick this up later in *Chapter 4, Exchange Security*. At this point, if you think you are
using the correct cmdlet to manage users in Exchange and it's not returning the result
that you expect, review *Chapter 4, Exchange Security* and come back to this section.

Creating a Mailbox for a new user

Some of the ways you can create mailboxes in Exchange 2013 are listed here:

- Create a new user in Active Directory and a new mailbox for the user
- Enable the mailbox for an existing user in the Active directory

Creating a new user in Active Directory and a new mailbox for the user

The new-mailbox cmdlet in Exchange 2013 and 2016 is used to create a new user in
the Active directory and a new mailbox on the Exchange 2013 server. For example,
the following command creates a mailbox for Frank Miller:

```
New-Mailbox -Alias Frankm -Name "Frank Miller" -FirstName Frank -LastName
Miller -DisplayName "Frank Miller" -UserPrincipalName frankm@contoso.
com -Password (ConvertTo-SecureString -String 'Pa$$word1' -AsPlainText
-Force)
```

Most of the parameters of the new-mailbox are self-explanatory, and you can use help to understand the syntax and parameters using `Get-help new-mailbox -detailed`.

The `ConvertTo-SecureString` function converts a plain text string called `Pa$$w0rd1` into a secure string that will be accepted by Windows PowerShell when creating a new user account in Active Directory. The cmdlet will create the user in the default **Organizational Unit (OU)**. If you want to create the user object in a specific OU, specify that you are using the `-OrganizationalUnit` parameter. If you notice carefully, the `-Database` option is not specified, but the cmdlet still succeeds in creating the new mailbox. This is possible due to the introduction of a new feature in the Exchange 2010 Service Pack 2 and later, called **Automatic mailbox distribution** feature, which will select a mailbox database to store the new or moved mailboxes. If you think this feature can create confusion in your Exchange Organization, it can be controlled using the role-based access control using Database management scopes, which we are going to cover in *Chapter 4, Exchange Security*.

Enabling mailbox for an existing user in Active directory

If you already have a user account in active directory and would like to create a mailbox for that user, `Enable-Mailbox` is the cmdlet for you. For example, the following cmdlet will enable the mailbox for Holly Holt on the database called `MailboxDatabase01`:

```
Enable-Mailbox holly@contoso.com -Database MailboxDatabase01
```

If you want to enable mailboxes for all the users, you can use the `Get-User` cmdlet to list and filter the users based on your requirement and then use pipe (|) to pass the output objects as input for the `Enable-Mailbox` cmdlet. For example, the following cmdlet will enable mailboxes for all users in the *Sales* department:

```
Get-user -Filter {Department -eq "Sales"} | Enable-Mailbox
```

Once the users are created in Active Directory with their mailbox enabled, you can then change any of the Active Directory properties using the `Set-User` cmdlet and exchange the related properties with the `Set-Mailbox` cmdlet.

The following cmdlet changes the department property of the users from sales to marketing and company attribute to Contoso:

```
Set-User -Identity Holly -Department Marketing -Company Contoso
```

Let's set the maximum message size that Holly can send to 3 MB:

```
Set-mailbox -identity holly -MaxSendSize 3145728
```

You can also run the cmdlets called `Set-User` and `Set-Mailbox` on multiple objects using the filtering capabilities of PowerShell and the usage of pipeline. The next example will change the issue Warning Quota, Prohibit Send Quota, and Prohibit Send Receive Quota to 3 GB, 4 GB, and 5 GB respectively to the users in the marketing organization unit. So, it will first warn the user that the mailbox is getting near the Quota at 3 GB but will still allow e-mail to be received and sent. After 4 GB, it will stop the user from sending emails and after 5 GB, both sending and receiving emails to and from these mailboxes will be stopped. Mailbox Quotas can also be applied on the Mailbox database on Exchange. The parameter called `UseDatabaseQuotaDefaults` is set to `False`, so the quota applied on the mailbox database will not be applicable for these users:

```
Get-Mailbox -OrganizationalUnit "Marketing" | Set-Mailbox -
IssueWarningQuota 3GB -ProhibitSendQuota 4GB -ProhibitSendReceiveQuota
5GB -UseDatabaseQuotaDefaults $false
```

Managing permissions

In this topic, we will look at ways by which we can assign permissions to users or groups called delegates. It allows the delegates to open and send messages from other mailboxes. Permissions can be assigned to mailboxes, distribution groups, and mail-enabled security groups. The following permissions can be assigned to delegates:

- **Full Access**: A delegate of a mailbox has full access to open a mailbox and access the content. This permission, however, will not allow the delegate to send mail from that mailbox.

- **Send As**: The Send As permission will allow the delegate to send messages from the other mailbox. The message in this case will appear to be coming from the mailbox owner. If Send As is used for a group, the message will appear to be originating from this group.

- **Send on Behalf**: This permission will also allow a delegate to send messages from other user's mailbox. Unlike the Send As permission, the message from this field will indicate that this message was sent by the delegate on behalf of the mailbox owner.

Manage Full Access permissions

The following example assigns the Full Access permission to Holly for Amy's mailbox:

```
Add-MailboxPermission -Identity "Amy Alberts" -User hollyh -AccessRights
FullAccess -InheritanceType all
```

If you are the administrator and there is a need to look at the content of some user's mailboxes, you can assign this permission using the following command. This example will provide full access permissions to admin@contoso.com for all the mailboxes:

```
Get-Mailbox -ResultSize unlimited -Filter {(RecipientTypeDetails -eq
'UserMailbox') -and (Alias -ne 'Admin')} | Add-MailboxPermission -User
admin@contoso.com -AccessRights fullaccess -InheritanceType all
```

You can view the Full Access permission using the following syntax:

```
Get-MailboxPermission -identity mailbox -User Delegate
```

For example, if you want to check if the permissions are set as per the first example, you need to type this:

```
Get-MailboxPermission -identity "Amy Alberts" -User hollyh
```

The Full Access permission, once granted, can be removed using the Remove-Mailbox permission. The following command will remove the full access granted to Holly Holt on Amy Albert's mailbox:

```
Remove-MailboxPermission -Identity "Amy Alberts" -User hollyh
-AccessRights FullAccess -InheritanceType All
```

Manage Send As permission

The Send As permission can be granted and revoked using the Add-AD and Remove-AD permissions. For example, the following command will assign the Send As permission to the Tier 1 Helpdesk Support Group on the shared mailbox of Helpdesk:

```
Add-ADPermission -Identity helpdeskshared -User Tier1helpdeskgroup
-ExtendedRights "Send As"
```

To view the permission, type this:

```
Get-ADPermission -identity helpdeskshared -User Tier1helpdeskgroup
```

If you are using Exchange Online, you need to replace -User with the -Trustee parameter.

The example removes the Send As permission for the user called John Doe from Holly Holt's mailbox:

```
Remove-ADPermission -Identity "Holly Holt" -User Johnd -ExtendedRights
"Send As"
```

Manage Send On Behalf permission

The Send on Behalf permission is managed using the Set-Mailbox cmdlet. The following cmdlet assigns the Send on Behalf to John Doe on Holly Holt's mailbox:

```
Set-Mailbox -Identity hollyh@contoso.com -GrantSendOnBehalfTo JohnD
```

The following command will remove the send on Behalf permission of the admin assistant group from the Executives shared mailbox:

```
Set-Mailbox "Executives" -GrantSendOnBehalfTo @{remove="adminassistant@
contoso.com"}
```

To view the send on behalf permission, type this:

```
Get-Mailbox -identity hollyh | FL GrantSendOnBehalfTo
```

Managing folder/calendar permission

In this topic, we will review the usage of folder permissions within a mailbox using PowerShell in Exchange 2013 and 2016 On-Premise and the Exchange Online environment. The three cmdlets that will help us to modify and view the permission on individual folders are Add-MailboxFolderPermission, Set-MailboxFolderPermission, Get-MailboxFolderPermission, and Remove-MailboxFolderPermission.

You can specify the following access rights using the Access Rights parameter, which are self-explanatory. If you want to understand about a particular access rights, type Get-Help Set-Mailbox folder permission. The access rights available are: Read Items, Create Items, Edit Owned Items, Delete Owned Items, Edit All Items, Delete All Items, Create Subfolders, Folder Owner, Folder Contact, and Folder Visible

There is a provision to specify a combination of the previously mentioned access rights by using: None, Owner, Publishing Editor, Editor, Publishing Author, Author, Non Editing Author, Reviewer, and Contributor.

For Calendars, we have two levels of access:

- **Availability Only**: This right will only show availability data.
- **Limited Details**: This will allow users to view the availability data along with its subject and location

The following command will add Amy Alberts as the Owner of the marketing folder in John Doe's mailbox:

```
Add-MailboxFolderPermission -Identity johnd@contoso.com:\Marketing -User
amya@contoso.com -AccessRights Owner
```

Now, the administrator who gave the permission earlier figured out that he wanted to only allow Amy as a Publishing Editor and not an owner. He will fix this using this command:

```
Set-MailboxFolderPermission -Identity johnd@contoso.com:\Marketing -User
amya@contoso.com -AccessRights PublishingEditor
```

Now, let's add Holly as the Publishing Editor for John Doe's calendar:

```
Add-MailboxFolderPermission Johnd:\calendar  -AccessRight
PublishingEditor -User hollyh
```

Similarly, add Holly to John's contact folder as a Publishing Editor:

```
Add-MailboxFolderPermission Johnd:\contacts -AccessRight PublishingEditor
-User hollyh
```

Now, let's view the results using the `Get-Mailbox Folder permission`. You can use the pipeline and select the desired results and even export it to a CSV file to review later:

```
Get-MailboxFolderPermission John:\calendar  | Select FolderName, user,
AccessRights
```

```
Get-MailboxFolderPermission John:\contacts
```

```
Get-MailboxFolderPermission John:\contacts  | Select FolderName, user,
AccessRights
```

```
Get-Mailbox | Get-MailboxFolderPermission | Export-CSV c:\temp\users.csv
```

Removing the permissions that are no longer required can be done by typing the following command:

```
Remove-MailboxFolderPermission Johnd:\calendar -User hollyh
-Confirm:$false
```

```
Remove-MailboxFolderPermission Johnd:\contacts -User hollyh
```

As an Exchange administrator, there are times when you want to remove a particular user's access from all the mailboxes for a particular folder, such as the calendar in this case. The unfortunate user is John Doe in this case. The first cmdlet called Get-Mailbox will return all the mailboxes in the Exchange organization, and you can filter this output using multiple attributes in the Active directory especially if you are managing a large organization with thousands of users. The output of `Get-Mailbox` will be fed into a `ForEach-Object` loop, and it will remove the permission from the calendar folder of each mailbox for the user John:

```
Get-Mailbox | ForEach-Object {Remove-MailboxFolderPermission $_":\
Calendar" -User Johnd} -Confirm:$False
```

Managing room mailboxes

The resource mailbox concept is not new in Exchange. Starting Exchange 2007, the concept of a room mailbox was introduced to allow users to book a meeting room, conference room, or training facility from their clients by inviting the room mailboxes in their meeting.

Let's create a room mailbox for the conference room on the first floor of Building 1. The mailbox will be located on Mailbox Database 1. The `-Room` parameter will define this mailbox as a Room Mailbox. The display name that users will see in the Global Address List is `Building 1—Conference Room 1`:

```
New-Mailbox -Database "Mailbox Database 1" -Name Bld1ConfRoom1 -
-DisplayName "Building 1 - Conference Room 1" -Room
```

You can view the settings of an existing room mailbox using this:

```
Get-Mailbox -identity Bld1ConfRoom1 | Format-List Name,
PrimarySMTPAddress, RecipientTypeDetails
```

If you have more than hundred room mailboxes in your organization, it will be easier to manage them by creating a room list. A room list is a specially flagged distribution used for managing rooms. For example, you may want to create a room list for all conference rooms with audio video conferencing equipment into one list and the rest into another list. This will help users to query the room list based on the usage of the equipment.

The following example will create a room list for all rooms with audio/video the conferencing equipment:

```
New-DistributionGroup -Name "AV Conference Rooms" -OrganizationalUnit
"contoso.com/rooms" -RoomList
```

Now, let's add the `Bld1ConfRoom1` room that we created earlier to the AV conference Rooms list:

```
Add-DistributionGroupMember -Identity "AV Conference Rooms" -Member
Bld1ConfRoom1 @contoso.com
```

You can use the `Set-DistributionGroup` cmdlet to change any existing distribution group to a room list:

```
Set-DistributionGroup -Identity "No AV Conference Rooms" -RoomList
```

There are properties of room mailboxes that can be classified into three categories and based on the categories; different cmdlets are used to manage them:

- **General**: This includes information about resource mailbox such as Name, Email Address, Capacity, Mailbox Database, Alias, Department, Company, Custom Attributes, and Hide from the address list setting. The `Get-User` and `Set-User` cmdlets are used to view and change the settings in this section.

- **Delegate**: This includes settings that will define how the room handles reservation requests, such as whether the booking will be handled automatically, or a delegate has to manually approve or decline meeting requests. This section also allows you to add and remove delegates for your room mailboxes. The `Set-Mailbox` and `Get-Mailbox` cmdlets are used to change the mailbox related properties such as Mailbox Database, Email Address, and more.

- **Booking Options**: This section will allow administrators to configure settings for the booking policy. Some of these settings are as follows:
    - Allow repeat meetings
    - Allow scheduling only during working hours
    - Always decline if the end date is beyond this limit
    - Maximum booking lead time (days)
    - Maximum duration (hours)

The cmdlets used to manage the booking options section are `Get-Calendar` Processing and `Set-Calendar` Processing.

The following example will set the general properties such as Display Name, Email Addresses, and Resource Capacity for a particular conference room:

```
Set-Mailbox "Bld2 Conference Room 2" -DisplayName "AV Conf Room 2/2 (20)"
-EmailAddresses SMTP:bld2conf2@contoso.com, smtp:bld2avconf2@contoso.com
-ResourceCapacity 20
```

The following command will use the pipeline to get all the room mailboxes and set the maximum time to 480 minutes (8 hours) for which the room can be booked:

```
Get-Mailbox -ResultSize unlimited -Filter {(RecipientTypeDetails -eq
'RoomMailbox')} | Set-CalendarProcessing -ScheduleOnlyDuringWorkHours
$true -MaximumDurationInMinutes 480
```

The following command will display the listed properties and their values for all the room mailboxes in your Exchange organization:

```
Get-Mailbox -ResultSize unlimited -Filter {(RecipientTypeDetails -eq
'RoomMailbox')} | Get-CalendarProcessing | | fl Identity,ScheduleOnlyDuri
ngWorkHours,MaximumDurationInMinutes
```

Import export of objects

As an Exchange administrator, you will be asked to create new users, contacts, and export content from Active Directory. This section will show you how to import and export objects to and from Active Directory.

Import user accounts in bulk using a CSV file

If you are an administrator tasked with adding lots of mailboxes for new users who have joined the company, you can use PowerShell to create these users in bulk.

First, you need a CSV file with the list of users that has to be created. The format of the CSV file will look like the following screenshot:

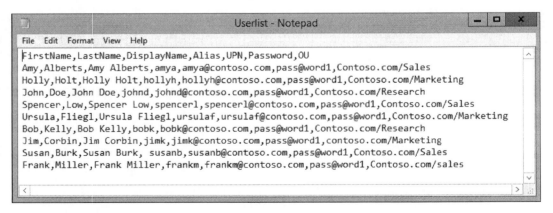

Save this file as UserList.csv.

The first line of the CSV file is important as it will indicate the corresponding values for the fields such as `FirstName`, `Alias`, and more for these users. Another thing to notice here is the presence of OU as I wanted to create these users in separate OUs in Active Directory. The password here is the same for simplicity, but it doesn't have to be this way; you can choose to use different passwords for different users.

The next step is to create a few variables to store the data that we will use in the script later. We will use the `$Database`, `$Password`, and `$Userlist` variables. The `$Password` variable will store the password and will use the `CovertTo-SecureString` function to convert plain text passwords into a secure string.

You need to check with your Exchange administrator to get the value of the `$Database` variable as all the mailboxes will be provisioned in this database, or you can choose the automatic mailbox distribution feature in Exchange 2013 that was explained earlier in this chapter. I am using the default database in Exchange 2013; and hence, you will see a random number at the end. You won't see this if you have a naming convention for your databases in your Exchange Organization.

The script will look as this. Save this script as `CreateMailboxes.ps1`:

```
$Database = "Mailbox Database 2020596250"
$Userlist = Import-CSV Userlist.csv
ForEach ($User in $Userlist)
{
$Password = ConvertTo-SecureString $User.Password -AsPlainText -Force
New-mailbox -Password $Password -Database $Database -UserprincipalName
$User.UPN -Alias $User.alias -Name $User.Displayname -FirstName $User.
Firstname -LastName $User.LastName -OrganizationalUnit $User.OU
}
```

Import external contacts in bulk using a CSV file

Another frequent request that Exchange and Active Directory administrators get is to import a list of contacts with the external email address from a file. In this section, we will talk about the process. Like we did while importing users, the first step is to create a CSV file with the following columns:

Save this file as `ExternalContacts.csv`. The next step is to create an Organizational Unit in Active Directory where these contacts will be imported. If you already have one created, skip this step.

The following command will take the input from the previous CSV file and create the contacts in the Contacts OU under `Contoso.com`:

```
Import-Csv Externalcontacts.csv | ForEach {New-MailContact -Name
$_.DisplayName -Firstname $_.FirstName -LastName $_.LastName
-ExternalEmailAddress $_.ExternalEmailAddress -OrganizationalUnit
contoso.com/contacts}
```

Exporting objects to a CSV file

At times, as an Active Directory or Exchange Administrator, you will be asked to export user objects to a CSV file. Here is a simple way to achieve this with a combination of `Get-ADUser`, `Select-Object`, and `Export-CSV` cmdlets. You can modify the properties that are selected based on your needs:

```
Get-ADUser -Filter * -Properties * | Select-Object -Property Name,SamAcco
untName,Description,EmailAddress,LastLogonDate,Manager,Title,Department,C
ompanywhenCreated,Enabled,MemberOf | Sort-Object -Property Name | export-
csv c:\temp\ADUsers.csv
```

Connecting from Remote computers

In order to manage Exchange servers, you don't need to install Exchange management tools on your computer or do a remote desktop connection to the Exchange server. All you need is Windows PowerShell on your local computer through which you can connect to a remote shell session on an Exchange server.

It is important to note that in order to connect to Exchange 2013 shell remotely, you can use either Window 8 or 8.1, Windows Server 2012, or 2012 R2. For Windows 7 SP1 and Windows 208 R2 SP1 to work, you need to install the .NET Framework 4.5 with either Windows Management Framework 3.0 or 4.0.

Connecting to a remote Exchange 2013/2016 Server

The first step is to use Windows PowerShell and type the following command:

```
$Credential = Get-Credential
```

This will pop up a Credential Request dialog box, you need to type the username and password of the user who has permission to manage Exchange.

The second step is to create a variable called `$Session` and store the configuration information using the `New-PSSession` cmdlet:

```
$Session = New-PSSession -ConfigurationName Microsoft.Exchange
-ConnectionUri http://<FQDN of Exchange 2013/2016 ClientAccess server>/
PowerShell/ -Authentication Kerberos -Credential $Credential
```

The next step is to import the `$Session` variable and you're done. You can start managing Exchange objects and servers right from the Windows PowerShell session:

```
Import-PSSession $Session
```

After you are done with your administration, ensure that you disconnect from your session. If you close the PowerShell Window without disconnecting, you might end up in a situation where all the remote sessions available to you are used. By default, every user gets a maximum of five sessions to a remote computer, and if you have used all five, then you will not be able to connect anymore. In such a case, use `Get-PSSession` to get a list of sessions and remove the unwanted session using the following command:

```
Remove-PSSession $Session
```

Connecting to Exchange online

You can use the same commands with a few URL modifications to connect to Exchange online. Here are the steps for it:

```
$Credential = Get-Credential
$Session = New-PSSession -ConfigurationName Microsoft.Exchange
-ConnectionUri https://outlook.office365.com/powershell-liveid/
-Credential $UserCredential -Authentication Basic -AllowRedirection
Import-PSSession $Session
```

Troubleshooting Remote PowerShell session connectivity

Here are a few tips that will help in troubleshooting if you are not able to connect to a remote Exchange server 2013/2016 `On-Premises` or Exchange Online:

- Check the username and password entered in the `$Credential` variable. A lot of time, it is due to a typing error while saving your credentials.

- Check whether your computer allows scripts to run using the Get-Execution policy, and if not, set it to `RemoteSigned`. This is covered in the *Writing a Basic Script* section in *Chapter 1, Getting Started with PowerShell* You need to type — `Set-ExecutionPolicy RemoteSigned`.

- Check whether the user who is trying to connect is enabled for using remote PowerShell. Run the command called `Get-User <username> | FL RemotePowerShellEnabled`. If the output is set to False, use `Set-User` to enable it and retry.

- For `on-premise` connectivity, you need Port 80 to be opened between your computer and Exchange server as you would have noticed by now that it is an HTTP connection. This is a note for administrators who are security conscious for the On-Premise connectivity of Exchange that happens over Kerberos, which encrypts the connection, and the data is not passed in clear text over the wire.

Mailbox reporting

In this section, we will review a simple example where certain selected or all the properties of mailbox objects can be exported to a CSV file for review. For instance, you are an administrator of a company who is planning to move to Exchange Online and wants to find out the mailbox sizes of the user mailboxes.

We will use a combination of `Get-Mailbox`, `Get-MailboxStatistics`, `Select-Object`, and `Export-CSV` cmdlets:

```
Get-Mailbox | Get-MailboxStatistics | Select-Object DisplayName,
ItemCount, TotalItemSize | Export-CSV "ExistingMailboxSize.csv"
```

Based on your requirements, you can build a complex script that can take multiple parameters as input, will do data conversion, and even send an email to specific people displaying the report in the HTML format. A simple example of a script is shared in the last topic of this chapter.

Automation with scripting agents

Cmdlet extension agents are introduced in Exchange Server 2010, and they are called when the Exchange 2010/2013/2016 cmdlets are executed. These agents are used to modify and extend the capabilities of cmdlets by performing additional tasks that the cmdlet alone cannot perform.

For example, in Exchange 2007, if you are using the New-Mailbox cmdlet without a `-Database` parameter, the command fails. However, if you use the same cmdlet in Exchange 2010/2013/2016 without the `-Database` parameter, a built-in cmdlet extension agent called Mailbox Resources Management is invoked. The agent will then automatically check for a mailbox database to create the mailbox and pass it on the `-Database` parameter.

One thing to note here is that the cmdlet extension agents can be invoked by the Exchange 2010/2013/2016 cmdlets only. Exchange 2007 or any third-party products cannot invoke these agents. Also these agents cannot be invoked through scripts. But if the scripts contain Exchange 2010/2013/2016 cmdlets, these agents will be called when executing those cmdlets.

In Exchange 2013/2016, there are these eight agents that can be invoked while executing a cmdlet. You will notice that all of these agents except the scripting agent are enabled by default. Agents cannot be added or removed from this list. However, you can use the Scripting agent to run PowerShell scripts to extend the functionality of cmdlets. These agents can be disabled and the priority can be changed except the ones that are listed as System agents. An agent's priority determines the order in which the agent is invoked. So, agents with lower priority number will be invoked first. Here is a list of default agents with their priority:

Agent name	Priority	Enabled by default	System agent
The Admin Audit Log agent	255	TRUE	Yes
The Scripting agent	6	FALSE	No
The Mailbox Resources Management agent	5	TRUE	No
The OAB Resources Management agent	4	TRUE	No
The Query-based DN agent	3	TRUE	No
The Provisioning Policy agent	2	TRUE	No
The Rus agent	1	TRUE	No
The Mailbox Creation Time agent	0	TRUE	No

Before you make any changes to the scripting agents and their priority, understand the impact it will have on the use of cmdlets on the Exchange servers in your organization.

When you have configured and enabled the scripting-agent extension agent, the cmdlets specified in the configuration XML file will check for some additional information and will set parameters or values specified in the configuration file in the following order:

- **Provision Default Properties:** As the name suggests, this API call is used to either set or override predefined values on object properties during creation of the objects. This will not impact the values of objects created or modified using higher priority agents.

- **Update Affected I Configurable:** If you need to set property values after all processing before invoking a valid API, you will use this API call. Again the values modified or set by higher priority agents is respected by this API.

- **Validate:** Just before the data gets written into the store, this API call is used to validate the property values on objects. Data gets written to the store if it succeeds and an error is returned, which is defined in this API if it fails.

- **OnComplete:** If you would like cmdlets to perform tasks after all the processing is complete, you will use this API call. For example, we will see how to provision an archive mailbox for users later in Scenario 1 and 2 using the OnComplete API.

Now, let's review the attributes of Scripting agent configuration file from the following table:

Element	Attribute	Description
Configuration	Not applicable	This element contains all the scripts that the Scripting agent cmdlet extension agent can run. The Feature tag is a child of this tag. There is only one Configuration tag in the configuration file.
Feature	Not applicable	This element contains a set of scripts that relate to a feature. Each script, defined in the ApiCall child tag, extends a specific part of the cmdlet execution pipeline. This tag contains the Name and Cmdlets attributes. There can be multiple Feature tags under the Configuration tag.
	Name	This attribute contains the name of the feature. Use this attribute to help identify which feature is extended by the scripts contained within the tag.
	Cmdlets	This attribute contains a list of the Exchange cmdlets used by the set of scripts in this feature extension. You can specify multiple cmdlets by separating each cmdlet with a comma.
ApiCall	Not applicable	This element contains scripts that can extend a part of the cmdlet execution pipeline. Each script is defined by the API call name in the cmdlet execution pipeline it's extending. The following are the API names that can be extended: Provision Default Properties Update AffectedIConfigurable Validate On Complete

Element	Attribute	Description
	Name	This attribute includes the name of the API call that's extending the cmdlet execution pipeline.
Common	Not applicable	This element contains functions that can be used by any script in the configuration file.

https://technet.microsoft.com/en-us/library/dd335054(v=exchg.150).aspx

The following two steps are required to enable the Scripting agent:

1. `ScriptingAgentConfig.xml.sample` in the `<Exchange Installation Path>\V15\Bin\CmdletExtensionAgents` file needs to be renamed to `ScriptingAgentConfig.xml` on every Exchange 2013/2016 server in your organization. You can make changes to this file on one server and copy it on all the Exchange 2013/2016 servers. The file has to be the same on all the servers; otherwise, inconsistent results will be returned based on the cmdlet execution and the server on which it was run.

2. `Enable-CmdletExtensionAgent "Scripting Agent"` will enable the scripting agent cmdlet extension agent.

Once the scripting agent is enabled, modify the file for the two scenarios.

Scenario 1

When any user mailbox is created, we disable ActiveSync, IMAP, and POP. By default, when you create a new mailbox, it enables ActiveSync, IMAP, and POP protocols.

You can check this by creating a new user through Exchange Admin Center or Exchange management Shell and use the following cmdlet:

```
PS C:\> Get-CASMailbox -Identity terrya

Name          ActiveSyncEnabled OWAEnabled   PopEnabled   ImapEnabled   MapiEnabled
----          ----------------- ----------   ----------   -----------   -----------
Terry Adams   True              True         True         True          True
```

Here is the content of the `ScriptingAgentConfig.xml` file. In this file, we will use the Mailbox provisioning feature and update the cmdlets that will be used to create (`New-Mailbox`) mailboxes:

```xml
<?xml version="1.0" encoding="utf-8" ?>
<Configuration version="1.0">
    <Feature Name="MailboxProvisioning" Cmdlets="New-Mailbox">
```

```
        <ApiCall Name="OnComplete">
          If($succeeded) {
            $mailbox = $provisioningHandler.
  UserSpecifiedParameters["Name"]
            Set-CASMailbox $mailbox -ActiveSyncEnabled $False
  -ImapEnabled $False -POPEnabled $False
                }
        </ApiCall>
      </Feature>
    </Configuration>
```

The $provisioningHandler.UserSpecified parameter contains user provided parameters passed to the cmdlet. $provisioningHandler. UserSpecifiedParameters["Name"] returns the value of the Name parameter in the New-Mailbox cmdlet.

Now, once the configuration file is set and you have enabled the cmdlet extension agent, it's time to test whether it works or not.

We will create a new mailbox for Peter and check the values of ActiveSync, POP, and IMAP, which should be disabled if the cmdlet extension agent is working. We will use the following cmdlet to create a new mailbox:

```
New-Mailbox -Alias peterh -Name "Peter Houston" -FirstName Peter
-LastName Houston -DisplayName "Peter Houston" -UserPrincipalName peterh@
contoso.com -Password (ConvertTo-SecureString -String 'pa$$word1'
-AsPlainText -Force)
```

Here is the result:

```
PS C:\> Get-CASMailbox -Identity peterh

Name            ActiveSyncEnabled OWAEnabled   PopEnabled   ImapEnabled   MapiEnabled
----            ----------------- ----------   ----------   -----------   -----------
Peter Houston   False             True         False        False         True
```

Scenario 2

Create an archive mailbox for all user mailboxes that are created. By default, you need to pass additional parameters to the New-Mailbox cmdlet to enable archive for a mailbox.

This is how your ScriptingAgentConfig.xml file will look for this scenario:

```
<?xml version="1.0" encoding="utf-8" ?>
<Configuration version="1.0">
    <Feature Name="MailboxProvisioning" Cmdlets="New-Mailbox">
      <ApiCall Name="OnComplete">
```

```
        If($succeeded) {
            $mailbox = $provisioningHandler.
    UserSpecifiedParameters["Name"]


            If ((Get-Mailbox $mailbox).ArchiveDatabase -eq $null)
        {

            Enable-Mailbox $mailbox -Archive
              }
          }
        </ApiCall>
      </Feature>
   </Configuration>
```

Now, it's time to test the cmdlet extension agent by creating a new mailbox. Remember, by default, New-Mailbox cmdlet will not create an archive mailbox. We will use the following command to create a new mailbox for Yan Li.

```
New-Mailbox -Alias yanl -Name "Yan Li" -FirstName Yan -LastName Li
-DisplayName "Yan Li" -UserPrincipalName yanl@contoso.com -Password
(ConvertTo-SecureString -String 'pa$$word1' -AsPlainText -Force)
```

The output of Get-Mailbox is listed here, which shows that an archive mailbox has been provisioned for Yan by the cmdlet Extension agent:

```
PS C:\> Get-Mailbox -Identity yanl | fl archive*

ArchiveDatabase      : MDB3
ArchiveGuid          : 487ff4c5-327c-4410-a4ad-6bac770c21b6
ArchiveName          : {In-Place Archive - Yan Li}
ArchiveQuota         : 100 GB (107,374,182,400 bytes)
ArchiveWarningQuota  : 90 GB (96,636,764,160 bytes)
ArchiveDomain        :
ArchiveStatus        : None
ArchiveState         : Local
ArchiveRelease       :
```

Writing a basic script

Now, let's use the knowledge that we have gained in the previous sections to write a script, and then we will schedule this script to run using the Windows task scheduler.

Let's try to understand the different sections of this script that will allow us to break the entire script into multiple parts, making it easier for us to understand the logic.

The first part defines parameters accepted by this script. Over here, we have defined the first parameter called `$ExportMailbox` to be a switch parameter, which is a mandatory one. A switch parameter means it is either true or false. In this case, this parameter has to be present as we have marked it as mandatory. If we use the script without this parameter, it will prompt, and it will fail if we don't specify it. The other two parameters will accept string values; and they are optional.

Next, we have used an If condition, which is true for `$ExportMailbox` as it is a mandatory parameter. It will initialize two variables. `$i` will be used as a counter and empty array `$Output`, which will be used to store the values later in the script.

Then, we have used the Test-Path cmdlet to check if the Path specified by the user exists; if not, it will create a directory in the specified path.

The next two lines will get the result for all the mailboxes or the mailbox whose identity has been specified by the user with the identity parameter. Notice that we have used this `!` (not operator) which means if identity parameter is not used, we get the result of all mailboxes:

```
if (! ($Identity)){$Mailboxes=Get-Mailbox -Filter
'RecipientTypeDetails -eq "UserMailbox"' -ResultSize unlimited}
```

If the identity parameter is used, get the result for only that mailbox. Another statement is used with the if statement here:

```
{$Mailboxes=$Identity|Get-Mailbox -Filter 'RecipientTypeDetails -eq
"UserMailbox"' -ResultSize unlimited}
```

The following code will increment the counter with every mailbox being processed and display a progress bar on the screen as a percentage of the completed mailboxes:

```
$i++

Write-Progress -Activity "Export Mailbox Statistics" -Status
"Exporting" -CurrentOperation $Mailbox.DisplayName -PercentComplete
($i/($Mailboxes.Count)*100)
```

Next, a ForEach loop is used to loop through each of the items in the variable `$Mailboxes`. A new variable called `$Mailboxstatistic` is used to create a new instance of a .NET Object. After this, we used the methods to convert the output displayed to Bytes and Megabytes using `TotalItemSize.Value.tobytes()` and `TotalItemSize.Value.toMB()`.

Add-Member is used to add new properties called `SamAccountName`, `DisplayName`, and `MailboxSizeinMB` properties to the objects stored in the `$MailboxStatistic` variable.

Next, we used an increment operator to store the values of $MailboxStatistic to initially define the empty array called $Output.

Finally, we use pipeline to feed the output of the array called $Output to Export-CSV to store in the log file path in the format of DD-MM-YYYY log. The Get-Date command is used to store the log files in a specific format.

Here is the script that you need to copy and save as mailboxstat.ps1.

This is how you will execute the script for all the mailboxes:

```
MailboxStat.ps1 -ExportMailbox
```

For a single mailbox, find the syntax here:

```
Mailboxstat.ps1 -ExportMailbox -Identity amya

    param
    (
            [Parameter(Mandatory=$true)][Switch] $ExportMailbox,

        [String] $LogPath="C:\temp\log",
        [String[]] $Identity


    )


    #Export today's report of User Mailbox Sizes
    if ($ExportMailbox)
    {
        $i=0
        $Output=@()
        if(! ( Test-Path -Path $LogPath)) {New-Item -ItemType  directory -Path $LogPath}

        #Get mailbox identity
        if (! ($Identity)){$Mailboxes=Get-Mailbox -Filter
'RecipientTypeDetails -eq "UserMailbox"' -ResultSize unlimited}

        else
        {$Mailboxes=$Identity|Get-Mailbox -Filter 'RecipientTypeDetails
-eq "UserMailbox"' -ResultSize unlimited}


        #Display SamAccountName,DisplayName and MailboxSizeinMB for users
with mailbox if no identity is specified, it will display sizes of all
mailboxes.
        foreach($Mailbox in $Mailboxes)
```

```
        {
            $i++
Write-Progress -Activity "Exporting Mailbox Statistics" -Status
"Exporting" -CurrentOperation $Mailbox.DisplayName -PercentComplete
($i/($Mailboxes.Count)*100)

            $MailboxStatistic = New-Object PSObject
            $MailboxSizeinBytes = (Get-MailboxStatistics -Identity
$Mailbox).TotalItemSize.Value.tobytes()
            $MailboxSizeinMB = (Get-MailboxStatistics -Identity $Mailbox).
TotalItemSize.Value.toMB()
            $MailboxStatistic | Add-Member -MemberType NoteProperty -Name
"SamAccountName" -Value $Mailbox.SamAccountName
            $MailboxStatistic | Add-Member -MemberType NoteProperty -Name
"DisplayName" -Value $Mailbox.DisplayName
            $MailboxStatistic | Add-Member -MemberType NoteProperty -Name
"MailboxSizeinMB" -Value $MailboxSizeinMB
            $Output += $MailboxStatistic
        }
    #Output to a CSV file will be in "dd-MM-yyyy" date format, in
default path "C:\temp\log". Path can be set by $logpath param.
    $Output|Export-Csv -Encoding default -NoTypeInformation -Path
"$LogPath\$(get-date -Format "dd-MM-yyyy").csv"
}
```

Scheduling your task

Now, let's schedule this script called `Mailboxstat.ps1` through the schedule task to run every day at midnight using the Windows task scheduler.

To run the Task Scheduler using the Windows interface, follow these steps:

Click on the Start button.

Click on Control Panel.

Click on Administrative Tools.

Double-click on Task Scheduler.

Click on Create task on the action menu.

Choose a name for the task and pick whether you want this task to run when the user is logged on or not.

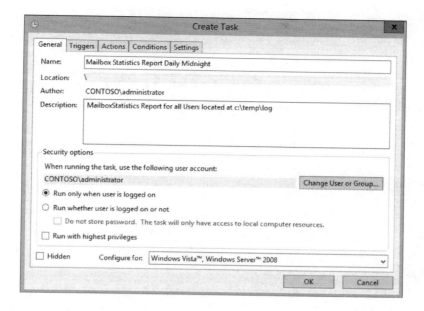

Open the **Triggers** tab and create a new trigger with your options and click on **OK** to create the trigger.

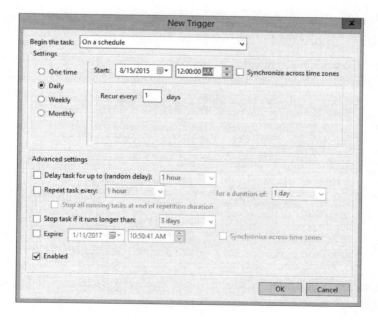

Click on the **Actions** tab and create a new action. Copy the following command to the "**Program/script**" textbox as shown in the following screenshot:

```
C:\Windows\System32\WindowsPowerShell\v1.0\powershell.exe -noexit
-command ". 'C:\Program Files\Microsoft\Exchange Server\V14\bin\
RemoteExchange.ps1'; Connect-ExchangeServer -auto; "&{C:\Scripts\
Mailboxstat.ps1 -ExportMailbox}"
```

You will get the following prompt once you click on **OK** as we have provided additional arguments for our script to execute. Click on **Yes** on the prompt here:

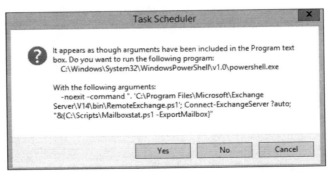

Now, you have a scheduled task that will run this script and export the report every day at midnight.

Summary

In this chapter, we covered recipient management that includes managing users and permissions and exporting and importing objects. We also covered ways to connect to remote Exchange servers through PowerShell and how to generate mailbox reports. Finally, we touched upon the concepts of scripting agents, which extend the functionality of Exchange cmdlets. We saw how to write a script and schedule it using the Task Scheduler.

In the next chapter, you will learn how to manage different types of distribution groups.

3
Handling Distribution Groups

This chapter is all about managing distribution groups as they play a major role in Exchange Administration. Administrators always spend a lot of time in adding/ removing members from distribution groups. Other management tasks include authorizing senders to a group. We will see how most of these tasks can be automated and how it can save a lot of time for administrators.

The following topics will be covered in this chapter:

- Introducing distribution groups
- Managing distribution groups
- Managing distribution group permissions
- Managing distribution group members
- Converting group types
- Automation with dynamic distribution groups
- Writing an advance script

Introducing distribution groups

The concept of group is not new to Active Directory administrators. Groups are a collection of user and computer accounts and other nested groups. Groups help us to make maintenance and administration easier.

From an Exchange administration perspective, these are the two groups that administrators have to deal with:

- **Distribution groups**: These groups can be used with applications that deal with e-mails to send it to a collection of users. To be specific, these are referred as mail-enabled universal distribution groups or simply distribution groups.

- **Security groups**: These groups are used to grant access permissions to resources in Active directory. These groups can also be mail enabled and used to distribute messages.

It is important to understand the difference between security and distribution groups. A distribution group does not have a security principal, which means it cannot be used to assign permissions to resources. It can only be used to send messages to a collection of users. On the other hand, a security group has a security context and is used to grant permission to resources. They can also be used to distribute messages if they are mail enabled, which is a process of adding additional properties to the group such as email addresses so that it can distribute emails to its members. As a best practice, we should only use distribution groups in Exchange, and this is what is going to be covered in the rest of this chapter except in the section called *Converting Group Types* where we talk about how to change the group types.

Managing distribution groups

Before we start talking about distribution group's management, we need to be aware of these first:

- **Recipient permissions**: You need to be assigned permissions before you can manage distribution groups. For details, review the section called *Managing distribution group permission* to understand role-based access control and its impact on the distribution group creation and modification.

- **The group naming policy**: If your organization has defined a naming policy for the created distribution groups, you need to review this. Since we are going to manage distribution groups using the Exchange Management shell, the naming policy will be applied unless you specify the -ignorenamingpolicy parameter to override the policy. If you are an administrator using **Exchange Admin Center** (**EAC**) to create distribution groups, the naming policy will be ignored.

Distribution Group naming policy

A distribution group naming policy will ensure that you have a consistent naming convention for your distribution groups created by your users. The following are the benefits of using a naming policy for distribution groups in your Exchange organization:

- It enforces consistent names being used to create distribution groups
- It can be used to identify the location, function, or type of users who are members of a particular group
- It prevents inappropriate words being used in group names

Let's create a distribution group naming policy using EAC. In this policy, we will create a policy that will have the prefix, `Contoso_DG` and `_Users` as a suffix to the group name:

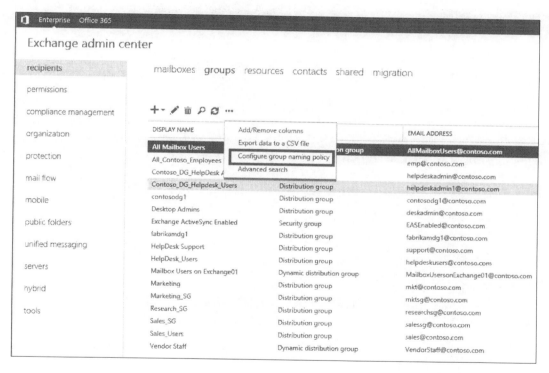

This will open the **Group Naming Policy** properties page and allow you to configure the options such as prefix, suffix, and blocked words.

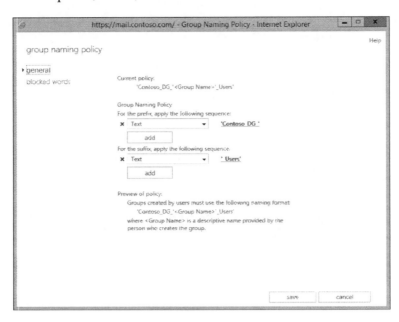

Since we are already using the prefix with words **dg** and **users**, we will put them in the blocked words list as shown in the following screenshot:

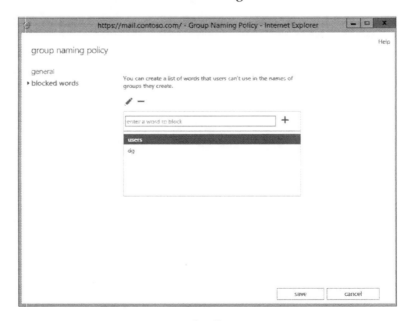

You can run the following command to get the group naming policy that you have just created:

```
Get-OrganizationConfig | FL DistributionGroupNamingPolicy.
```

Creating Distribution Groups

Now, let's test whether our new group naming policy is working or not by creating a new distribution group for the HelpDesk administrators:

```
New-DistributionGroup -Name "HelpDesk_Administrators" -Alias
helpdeskadmin
```

With the following command, you can view the Name and DisplayName properties and verify that Contoso_DG and _Users have been added as a prefix and suffix respectively:

```
Get-DistributionGroup Contoso_DG_HelpDesk_Administrators_Users | FL Name,
DisplayName
```

Now, let's try to override the naming policy by creating another distribution group using the –ignorenamingpolicy parameter:

```
New-DistributionGroup -Name "Desktop Admins" -Alias deskadmin -
IgnoreNamingPolicy
```

Now, let's use one of the words that we have blocked while creating a new distribution group:

```
New-DistributionGroup -Name "HelpDesk_Users" -Alias helpdeskusers
```

You will get the following error message:

```
PS C:\> New-DistributionGroup -Name "HelpDesk_Users" -Alias helpdeskusers
The group name contains the word "users", which isn't allowed in group names in your
organization. Please rename your group.
    + CategoryInfo          : NotSpecified: (:) [New-DistributionGroup], DataValidationExcepti
on
    + FullyQualifiedErrorId : [Server=EXCHANGE01,RequestId=dce67823-c9a2-40a8-8b9a-a3b16045512
8,TimeStamp=1/11/2016 11:00:46 AM] [FailureCategory=Cmdlet-DataValidationException] 7E06F3
22,Microsoft.Exchange.Management.RecipientTasks.NewDistributionGroup
    + PSComputerName        : exchange01.contoso.com
```

At this point, you can change the name of the distribution group or use the –IgnorenamingPolicy parameter to override the group naming policy.

Changing Distribution Group properties

Once a distribution group is created, you can manage them either through Exchange Admin center or Exchange Management Shell cmdlets. The following sections are available for Distribution Group Properties:

- **General**: This section allows you to view/modify the Display Name, Alias, Description, Organizational Unit, and Hide from address lists settings.

- **Ownership**: Group owners can be assigned using this tab, who can then approve or reject requests to join or leave this group. The owners can also act as moderators for emails sent to this group by approving or rejecting the messages. The user who creates a group by default becomes the group owner.

- **Membership**: Distribution group membership can be managed using this section.

- **Membership approval**: This section specifies whether an approval is required to join or leave a group or whether the group is open or not (which means no approval is required).

- **Delivery management**: This section is used to define who sends the message to a particular distribution group. You can choose a distribution group to only accept messages from internal users or both internal and external users. If you choose the latter, you can also specify a list of users who can send emails. Emails for all other users to this group will be rejected.

- **Message approval**: This section allows you to specify moderation settings. You will get an option to enable moderation for a group, select group moderators, and exceptions (users whose messages to the groups do not need approvals). You can also specify moderation notification to be sent to all senders, to senders inside the organization or don't send it at all.

- **Email options**: This section allows you to view or modify the email addresses assigned to a distribution group.

- **MailTip**: You can configure MailTip, which is an alert displayed when someone uses this distribution group in an email in the To, Cc, or Bcc line.

- **Group delegation**: This section is used to assign permission to a user that will allow them to send messages as the group itself (Send As) or send messages on behalf of the group.

For example, the following command changes the primary and secondary SMTP addresses for the `All_Contoso_Employees` group:

```
Set-DistributionGroup "All_Contoso_Employees" -EmailAddresses
SMTP:allemployees@contoso.com,smtp:employees@contoso.com
```

The example limits the message size for all distribution groups to 5 MB:

```
Get-DistributionGroup -ResultSize unlimited -Filter
{(RecipientTypeDetails -eq 'MailUniversalDistributionGroup')} | Set-
DistributionGroup -MaxReceiveSize 5MB
```

This example enables moderation for the distribution group Helpdesk Support and sets the moderator to Amy Albert. This will also notify senders who send mail from within the organization if their messages are not approved:

```
Set-DistributionGroup -Identity "Helpdesk Support" -ModeratedBy "Amy
Alberts" -ModerationEnabled $true -SendModerationNotifications 'Internal'
```

The following example requires the owner of the group called Exchange Enthusiasts to approve a user's request to join this group:

```
Set-DistributionGroup -Identity "Exchange Enthusiasts"
-MemberJoinRestriction 'ApprovalRequired'
```

Managing distribution group permissions

In the Exchange server releases prior to Exchange 2010, in order to allow a user to manage a distribution group, we just had to add the user to the distribution group owner. This changed with Exchange 2010; and later, it was released due to the introduction of a new model of delegation called **role-based access control** (**RBAC**).

Due to the introduction of RBAC in Exchange 2010 and later, if you assign the owner permission to a user for a distribution group and he tries to modify the membership of the group through Outlook, the user will get the following error:

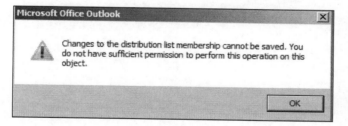

In order to fix this issue, we need to understand how the RBAC model works. We will review RBAC from a distribution group management perspective here, and later on in *Chapter 4, Exchange Security* we will take a deep dive into the concepts.

RBAC enables administrators to control delegation at a very granular level; this is something that other specialist users, helpdesk administrators, and end users can also do. Prior to Exchange 2010, we used to rely on Active Directory Access Control Lists (ACLs), which was difficult to manage and troubleshoot.

In Exchange 2010, with RBAC, we are able to control both: the administrative tasks that can be performed and the extent to which users can now administer their own mailboxes and distribution groups.

There are two primary ways to assign permissions to your users in your organization. These are through management role groups and assignments. Each of these methods will associate users with the permissions that they need to perform their tasks.

With RBAC, we have an option to use the built-in roles that come with the Exchange installation or customize the built-in role to satisfy our needs.

Let's first review the RBAC role used to manage distribution groups by the end users. For this, you need to look at **Default Role Assignment Policy** in Exchange Admin Center. You will find it under the **permissions** section in the user roles tab as shown in the following screenshot:

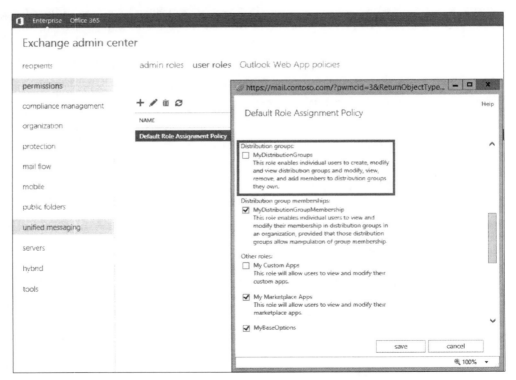

By default, the RBAC role called `MyDistributionGroups` is not added to the default policy. If you check this box, it will allow users to create, view, and modify the distribution groups and its members for the groups they own.

Now, let's review the cmdlets that are available to the role called `MyDistributionGroups`. Open the Exchange Management shell, and type the following command to list all the cmdlets available for this role:

```
Get-ManagementRoleEntry "MyDistributionGroups\*"
```

The result is shown in the following screenshot:

```
PS C:\> Get-ManagementRoleEntry "MyDistributionGroups\*"

Name                          Role                   Parameters
----                          ----                   ----------
Update-DistributionGroupMember MyDistributionGroups  {Confirm, ErrorAction, ErrorVariable,
Set-Group                     MyDistributionGroups   {DisplayName, ErrorAction, ErrorVarial
Set-DynamicDistributionGroup  MyDistributionGroups   {ErrorAction, ErrorVariable, Identity
Set-DistributionGroup         MyDistributionGroups   {AcceptMessagesOnlyFrom, AcceptMessage
Remove-DistributionGroupMember MyDistributionGroups  {Confirm, ErrorAction, ErrorVariable,
Remove-DistributionGroup      MyDistributionGroups   {Confirm, ErrorAction, ErrorVariable,
New-DistributionGroup         MyDistributionGroups   {Alias, Confirm, CopyOwnerToMember, D
Get-Recipient                 MyDistributionGroups   {Anr, BookmarkDisplayName, ErrorActio
Get-Group                     MyDistributionGroups   {Anr, ErrorAction, ErrorVariable, Fil
Get-DistributionGroupMember   MyDistributionGroups   {ErrorAction, ErrorVariable, Identity
Get-DistributionGroup         MyDistributionGroups   {Anr, ErrorAction, ErrorVariable, Fil
Add-DistributionGroupMember   MyDistributionGroups   {Confirm, ErrorAction, ErrorVariable,
```

As you can see in the output, the users who are assigned to this role can also create and remove distribution groups, which might not me a desirable permission to be granted to all end users.

RBAC allows you to customize the built-in roles. We will see how the `MyDistributionGroups` role can be customized for end users to be able to manage the distribution groups that they own. But, they will not be able to create or remove distribution groups.

The default role groups are read only and cannot be modified; hence, we need to create a new role under `MyDistributionGroups`, which will inherit `ManagementRoleEntries` from the parent. Then, we will customize the newly created role and associate it with `Default Role Assignment Policy`. We will call the new role as `ContosoDGManagement`:

```
New-ManagementRole -Name ContosoDGManagement -Parent
"MyDistributionGroups"
```

If you run the following cmdlet, you will find that the new role called `ContosoDGManagement` has inherited all the management role entries (which are cmdlets associated with this role):

```
Get-ManagementRoleEntry "ContosoDGManagement\*"
```

Now, the next step is to decide what cmdlets should be made available to this new role.

Scenario

The Contoso management has decided to allow users to add only distribution group members. All other administration will be done by HelpDesk and Exchange administrators. As we are creating this role for the end users, we will remove all the cmdlets that will allow users to change the distribution group properties, and we will remove members from the newly created role called ContosoDGManagement.

The following command will remove the cmdlets starting with Set-*. In other words, it will prevent users from modifying the distribution groups using the Set-Group, Set-DyanamicDistributionGroup and Set-DistributionGroup cmdlets:

```
Get-ManagementRoleEntry "ContosoDGManagement\set-*" | Remove-
ManagementRoleEntry -Confirm:$false
```

Now, let's remove the cmdlets that will prevent users from creating new distribution groups:

```
Get-ManagementRoleEntry "ContosoDGManagement\New-*" | Remove-
ManagementRoleEntry -Confirm:$false
```

We also need to ensure that end users should not be able to remove the existing distribution groups:

```
Get-ManagementRoleEntry "ContosoDGManagement\Remove-DistributionGroup" |
Remove-ManagementRoleEntry -Confirm:$false
```

Once we have customized the management role, we can view the role entries using the following command:

```
Get-ManagementRoleEntry "ContosoDGManagement\*"
```

The following screenshot is what you get:

```
PS C:\> Get-ManagementRoleEntry "ContosoDGManagement\*"

Name                             Role                   Parameters
----                             ----                   ----------
Add-DistributionGroupMember      ContosoDGManagement    {Confirm, ErrorAction, ErrorVariable,
Get-DistributionGroup            ContosoDGManagement    {Anr, ErrorAction, ErrorVariable, Fil
Get-DistributionGroupMember      ContosoDGManagement    {ErrorAction, ErrorVariable, Identity
Get-Group                        ContosoDGManagement    {Anr, ErrorAction, ErrorVariable, Fil
Get-Recipient                    ContosoDGManagement    {Anr, BookmarkDisplayName, ErrorActio
Remove-DistributionGroupMember   ContosoDGManagement    {Confirm, ErrorAction, ErrorVariable,
Update-DistributionGroupMember   ContosoDGManagement    {Confirm, ErrorAction, ErrorVariable,
```

Now, we have customized the management role called ContosoDGManagement as per our requirements. The next step is to add this to the Default Role Assignment Policy, which will grant only what is specified in the ContosoDGManagement Role as seen in the following screenshot:

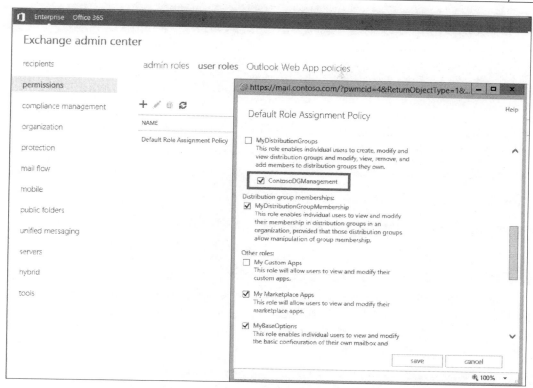

Users will now be able to add and remove the distribution group members that they own as seen in the following screenshot:

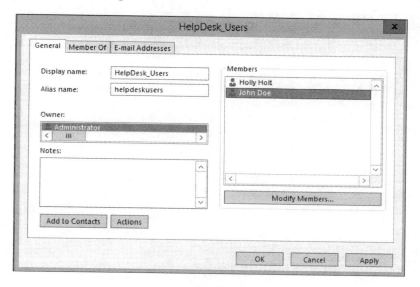

Managing distribution group members

This following example adds Holly Holt to a distribution group called `Helpdesk_Users`:

```
Add-DistributionGroupMember -Identity "Helpdesk_Users" -Member "hollyh@
contoso.com"
```

If you need to display the list of users who are the members of marketing users group, type the following:

```
Get-DistributionGroupMember -Identity "Marketing"
```

Now, let's remove John Doe from the Marketing group:

```
Remove-DistributionGroupMember -Identity "Marketing" -Member "John Doe"
```

Converting group types

We have reviewed the group types in Active Directory earlier in this chapter. At a high level, there are two types of groups—Security and Distribution. Both Security and Distribution groups can be email enabled and used to distribute emails to a collection of users and groups.

You need to be careful while using security groups for email distribution as these groups have security principals, and you may unintentionally grant a user or group permission to access a resource such as the file share assigned to this group. As a best practice, only distribution groups should be used for emails.

To convert the existing security into distribution groups, you will need the Active Directory PowerShell module, which is available on Windows 2008 R2 and later versions. To get a list of available modules, type `Get-Module -ListAvailable`.

The following command will import the `ActiveDirectory` module:

```
Import-Module ActiveDirectory
```

Before making any changes to the group type, ensure that a particular security group is not used to assign permission to resources.

Let's review the properties of a group called `Sales_Users` using Active Directory where users are computers, with the help of the following screenshot:

The following command will change the `Sales_Users` Security group to a distribution group. The `-GroupCategory` parameter accepts two values— `0` for the distribution group and 1 for the security group:

```
Set-ADGroup Sales_Users -GroupCategory 0
```

The same result can be achieved using Active Directory users and computers. Here is the result of previous command:

If you are looking to convert all of your mail enabled security groups to distribution groups, you can use the `Get-DistributionGroup` cmdlet in exchange and pipe the output to `Set-ADGroup`.

Here is an example:

```
Get-DistributionGroup -RecipientTypeDetails MailUniversalSecurityGroup |
Foreach-Object {$Group=$_; Write-Host $Group.Name; Write-Host "Converting
Security Groups to Distribution Groups… "; Set-ADGroup $Group.
DistinguishedName -GroupCategory 0}
```

Automation with dynamic Distribution groups

A dynamic distribution group is a special type of distribution group where members are not static. The membership of a dynamic distribution group is calculated every time an email is sent to the group. The membership of a dynamic distribution group is defined by a filter or a condition defined by the administrator or owner.

In other words, you will not find any members in a dynamic distribution group property. Instead, you will see a filter or condition specified in the membership section. All the objects that satisfy the condition will receive an email sent to the dynamic distribution group.

The following example creates the dynamic distribution group called "All Mailbox Users" that contains only mailbox users:

```
New-DynamicDistributionGroup -IncludedRecipients MailboxUsers -Name "All
Mailbox Users" -OrganizationalUnit Users
```

The following example creates a dynamic distribution group with a custom recipient filter. The dynamic distribution group contains all the mailbox users on a server called Exchange01:

```
New-DynamicDistributionGroup -Name "Mailbox Users on Exchange01"
-OrganizationalUnit Users -RecipientFilter {((RecipientTypeDetails -eq
'UserMailbox' -and ServerName -eq 'Exchange01'))}
```

The following example creates a dynamic distribution group with a custom recipient filter. The dynamic distribution group contains all the mailbox users that have a value of Vendor in the CustomAttribute5 property:

```
New-DynamicDistributionGroup -Name "Vendor Staff" -RecipientFilter
{(RecipientTypeDetails -eq 'UserMailbox') -and (CustomAttribute5 -eq
'Vendor')}
```

The following example displays the list of all dynamic distribution groups with properties:

```
Get-DynamicDistributionGroup | FL Name,RecipientTypeDetails,RecipientFilt
er,PrimarySmtpAddress
```

Dynamic Distribution group properties

Following are the properties of Dynamic Distribution group:

- **General**: This section allows you to view/modify Display Name, Alias, Description, Organizational Unit, and Hide from address lists settings.

- **Ownership**: A dynamic distribution group can have only one owner, which is displayed in the Managed by tab of the group properties when viewed through Active Directory users and computers.

- **Membership**: This section is used to change the filter that defines who will be the member of this particular dynamic distribution group.

- **Delivery management**: This section is used to define who sends the message to a particular distribution group. You can choose a distribution group to only accept messages from internal users or both internal and external users. If you choose the latter, you can also specify a list of users who can send emails. Emails for all other users to this group will be rejected.

- **Message approval**: This section allows you to specify moderation settings. You will get an option to enable moderation for a group and select group moderators and exceptions (users whose message to the groups do not need an approval). You can also specify moderation notification to be sent to all senders and to senders inside the organization or don't send it at all.

- **Email options**: This section allows you to view or modify the email addresses assigned to a distribution group.

- **MailTip**: You can configure MailTip, which is an alert displayed when someone uses this distribution group in an email in the To, Cc, or Bcc line.

- **Group delegation**: This section is used to assign permission to a user that will allow them to send messages as the group itself (Send As) or send messages on behalf of the group.

The following example hides all the dynamic distribution groups from address list and sets the maximum size of the email to be received as 10 MB. It also sets moderation for these groups and sets administrator as the moderator:

```
Get-DynamicDistributionGroup -ResultSize unlimited | Set-
DynamicDistributionGroup -HiddenFromAddressListsEnabled $true
-MaxReceiveSize 10MB -ModerationEnabled $true -ModeratedBy administrator
```

The following example sets the primary SMTP address for the All Mailbox Users dynamic distribution group to `All.Users@contoso.com`:

```
Set-DynamicDistributionGroup -Identity "All Mailbox Users"
-EmailAddresses SMTP:All.users@contoso.com
```

The following example displays the results of all the dynamic distribution groups with properties:

```
Get-DynamicDistributionGroup -ResultSize unlimited | fl Name,HiddenFromAd
dressListsEnabled,MaxReceiveSize,ModerationEnabled,ModeratedBy
```

Writing an advance script

The following script will ask for inputs from the user and display the distribution group membership report either on the console or redirect it to a CSV file based on the selected option. The full script can be found at the TechNet Script center at `https://gallery.technet.microsoft.com/office/Export-all-distribution-707c27eb` written by Satheshwaran Manoharan.

In this script, a `Switch` statement is used to check two conditions. A few variables and an empty array called `$Displayout` has been declared, which are used later in the script to store the output that is redirected to a CSV file based on the user's inputs. The New-Object cmdlet is used to create a new instance of the Windows PowerShell object and add the required custom properties using the Add-member cmdlet.

In the second section, the results have been added to the empty array that we have declared `$Displayout`, which will be piped to the Export-CSV cmdlet to export the output to a CSV file.

Finally, if the script doesn't detect an input, the default section at the end of the script will be executed and will ask you to enter the inputs in RED:

```
Write-host "
Distribution Group Membership Report
=====================================
1.Display in Exchange Management Shell Console
2.Export to CSV File"
#========
#Script
#========

Write-Host "                        "

$TaskNo = Read-Host "Choose The Task"
$Displayout = @()
switch ($TaskNo)

{
```

```
1 {

$alldg = Get-DistributionGroup -resultsize unlimited

Foreach($dg in $alldg)

{

$DGMembers = Get-DistributionGroupMember $dg.name -resultsize
unlimited

$MemberCount = $DGMembers.Count

$Counter = $MemberCount-1

For($i=0;$i -le $Counter;$i++)

{

$NewObject = New-Object PSObject

$NewObject | Add-Member NoteProperty -Name "DisplayName" -Value
$DGmembers[$i].Name
$NewObject | Add-Member NoteProperty -Name "Alias" -Value
$DGmembers[$i].Alias
$NewObject | Add-Member NoteProperty -Name "Primary SMTP address"
-Value $DGmembers[$i].PrimarySmtpAddress
$NewObject | Add-Member NoteProperty -Name "Distribution Group" -Value
$DG.Name


Write-Output $NewObject

}

}

;Break}

2 {

$CSV = Read-Host "Enter the Path of CSV file (Eg. C:\DGMember.csv)"

$AllDG = Get-DistributionGroup -resultsize unlimited
```

```
Foreach($dg in $allDg)

{

$DGMembers = Get-DistributionGroupMember $Dg.name -resultsize
unlimited

$MemberCount = $DGMembers.Count

$Counter = $MemberCount-1

For($i=0;$i -le $Counter;$i++)

{


$NewObject = New-Object PSObject

$NewObject | Add-Member NoteProperty -Name "DisplayName" -Value
$DGmembers[$i].Name
$NewObject | Add-Member NoteProperty -Name "Alias" -Value
$DGmembers[$i].Alias
$NewObject | Add-Member NoteProperty -Name "RecipientType" -Value
$DGmembers[$i].RecipientType
$NewObject | Add-Member NoteProperty -Name "Recipient OU" -Value
$DGmembers[$i].OrganizationalUnit
$NewObject | Add-Member NoteProperty -Name "Primary SMTP address"
-Value $DGmembers[$i].PrimarySmtpAddress
$NewObject | Add-Member NoteProperty -Name "Distribution Group" -Value
$DG.Name
$NewObject | Add-Member NoteProperty -Name "Distribution Group Primary
SMTP address" -Value $DG.PrimarySmtpAddress
$NewObject | Add-Member NoteProperty -Name "Distribution Group OU"
-Value $DG.OrganizationalUnit
$NewObject | Add-Member NoteProperty -Name "Distribution Group Type"
-Value $DG.GroupType
$NewObject | Add-Member NoteProperty -Name "Distribution Group
Recipient Type" -Value $DG.RecipientType


$Displayout += $NewObject

}
```

```
$Displayout | Export-csv -Path $CSV -NoTypeInformation

}

;Break}

Default {Write-Host "No inputs found , Enter your options" -ForeGround
"red"}


}
```

Summary

In this chapter, we covered the concepts of groups from an Active Directory and Exchange perspective and their usage in different scenarios. Management of distribution groups with their permissions was also reviewed along with the usage of dynamic distribution groups and how to change the group types.

In the next chapter, we will look at how to secure Exchange deployments.

4
Exchange Security

Role-based access control (RBAC) is the new permissions model introduced in Exchange 2010. In the earlier versions of Exchange prior to Exchange 2010, we used to manage permissions on Exchange objects through Active Directory access control lists (ACLs). Modifying ACLs can have serious consequences from a management and upgrade perspective and can get complex very quickly.

RBAC provides a framework that allows delegation in Exchange Organization.

In this chapter, we will talk about securing Exchange and delegating access to administration tasks using RBAC. We will also configure certificates on Exchange and review its usage. The next configuration of applications to relay e-mails through Exchange will also be covered in this chapter. We will end this chapter by reviewing how to allow and block administrators to manage Exchange using Exchange Admin Center from the external network.

The following topics will be covered in this chapter:

- The components of RBAC
- Managing RBAC
- Creating and managing Custom Role Groups
- Managing Exchange Certificates
- Managing Application Relaying emails.
- Managing External Access of Exchange Admin Center
- Writing a basic script

Components of Role Based Access Control

Let's first review the components of Role Based Access Control (RBAC)

- **The management role group**: This is a universal security group (USG), which is flagged to be used by RBAC and contains mailboxes, users, and other USGs. This is used for role assignment.

- **The management role:** A management role is a container object that stores a list of cmdlets or scripts for a specific task in Exchange, for example, recipient management. The list of cmdlets and scripts are called as management role entries.

- **The management role scope**: This is an object that defines the scope on which the management role can have an impact. For example, it could be users within a specific group or organizations unit, a filtered list of databases, servers, or recipients.

- **The management role assignment**: This is an object that glues together a management role with a role group and scope. Management role assignments are created when we assign a role to a role group and a scope, which allows users in this particular role group to perform tasks defined in the management role on objects defined in the management scope.

Managing Role Based Access Control

Let's try to understand the different components of RBAC in the following triangle:

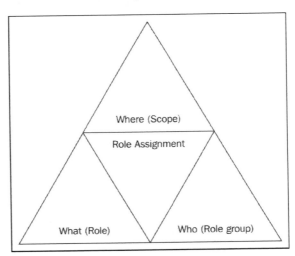

You will now explore into managing role-based access control in depth, so let's see what's in store for you.

Where (scope)

This defines where the assignment that you are going to define work. It could be on a particular organizational unit, a group of users, or even objects in the configuration container, such as a group of Exchange servers or specific databases.

Each RBAC role has its recipient read and write scope and a configuration read write scope. The built-in management roles have these scopes assigned implicitly. To get a list of the implicit scopes for the default RBAC roles, type the following command:

```
Get-ManagementRole | FL Name, *Scope*
```

As we have covered in *Chapter 3, Handling Distribution Groups,* if you would like to modify any of the default RBAC roles, you have to create a `New role`, which is a child of one of these default roles. Then, modify this child role. This is because RBAC will not allow you to modify any of the default roles available. If you have not specified the scope when you defined the new child role, it will inherit the implicit scope for the parent.

The following example will create a new scope for the sales user:

```
New-ManagementScope -name "Sales Users" -RecipientRestrictionFilter
{memberofgroup -eq "CN=Sales_Users,OU=Sales,DC=contoso,DC=com"}
```

Now, let's take a look at another example that will allow you to set the scope in the configuration container. For example, the following command will create a new management scope, which when applied, will restrict administrators to making changes to specific objects in the configuration container. Here, a list of Exchange servers used where administrators can make changes to whether this scope is applied to their management roles. They will not be able to make changes to other Exchange servers in the organization. This is handy if you have a global organization and would like to restrict access for regional administrators to servers within their region:

```
New-ManagementScope -Name "Exchange Servers in APAC" -ServerList APJ-
Ex01,APJ-Ex02,APJ-Ex03
```

You can also specify Exchange databases in your scope that you would like your Helpdesk or specialist users to work on.

Now that the scope is defined, let's move onto the *what* part where we will see what tasks can be performed.

What (role)

Now, you know where the role is going to act as you have defined the scope (where). Now is the time to decide what the role is going to do. By default, Exchange 2010/2013 comes with a large number of built-in roles (yes, they do!). Each of these roles is created to cover a given set of tasks. If you feel that your requirements are different and you would like to customize one of these roles, you just need to create a child role and remove the extra permissions that you feel are not required in your environment.

You can control what a role can or cannot do by modifying the cmdlets and parameters that are on the role. For example, the following command will display a list of cmdlets and their parameters that are available to the Mail Recipients role:

```
Get-ManagementRoleEntry -Role "Mail Recipients\*"
```

Now, let's create a new role that will only be able to modify properties such as City, Office, Phone, Mobile phone, Department, Postal Code, and Manager attributes for the users. These are the parameters for the Set-User cmdlet. So, we are going to create a new management role that will be the child of Mail recipients, and we are going to remove all the other parameters except Get-User and Set-User with the previous parameter.

Here are the commands that we are going to execute:

```
New-ManagementRole -Name "HelpDesk" -Parent "Mail Recipients"
```

```
Get-ManagementRoleEntry "HelpDesk\*" | Where {$_.name -ne "Get-User"} |
Remove-ManagementRoleEntry
```

```
Add-ManagementRoleEntry "HelpDesk\Set-User" -Parameters Office,City,Posta
lCode,Phone,Mobilephone,Department,Manager
```

This will allow any user who has the Helpdesk role assigned to modify the Active Directory properties listed in the Set-User parameter.

Now that we have looked at the where and what part of the triangle, let's review the who part.

Who (Role Group)

This defines the people who are going to get access to the role defined by what and the scope defined by where. This is called the Management role group which is a specially flagged universal security group

The following command will list the built in Exchange role groups

```
Get-RoleGroup
```

And here's what you get. (Pun intended!)

```
PS C:\> Get-RoleGroup

Name                              AssignedRoles              RoleAssignments
----                              -------------              ---------------
Organization Management           {Active Directory Permissi... {Active Directory Permissi...
Recipient Management              {Distribution Groups, Mail... {Distribution Groups-Recip...
View-Only Organization Man...     {Monitoring, View-Only Con... {Monitoring-View-Only Orga...
Public Folder Management          {Mail Enabled Public Folde... {Mail Enabled Public Folde...
UM Management                     {UM Mailboxes, UM Prompts,... {UM Mailboxes-UM Managemen...
Help Desk                         {User Options, View-Only R... {User Options-Help Desk, V...
Records Management                {Audit Logs, Journaling, M... {Audit Logs-Records Manage...
Discovery Management              {Legal Hold, Mailbox Search} {Legal Hold-Discovery Mana...
Server Management                 {Database Copies, Database... {Database Copies-Server Ma...
Delegated Setup                   {View-Only Configuration}  {View-Only Configuration-D...
Hygiene Management                {ApplicationImpersonation,... {ApplicationImpersonation-...
Compliance Management             {Data Loss Prevention, Inf... {Data Loss Prevention-Comp...
```

This will list the default role group that ships with Exchange and allows you to handle the most common administrative tasks for most customers.

Let's create a new role group, which will define "who" can work with our new role Helpdesk (which defines the what), and the management role scope of sales Users (which defines the where). We have used this example to tie all this together:

```
New-RoleGroup "Helpdesk for Sales Department" -Roles "Helpdesk"
-CustomRecipientWriteScope "Sales Users"
```

When a role group is created, at least one role must be assigned to this group. Multiple roles can be assigned to a role group if you want the members of the role group to perform more than one task.

Role assignment

The Where (Scope), What (Role) and Who (Role Group) are all Active directory objects. Role assignment is another Active Directory object that links all these together.

In the previous example where we have used the `New-RoleGroup` cmdlet, it created a Role assignment policy that links the Role (what) with the Scope (where) and the Role group (who). If you execute the following cmdlet, it will list all the role assignments:

```
Get-ManagementRoleAssignment
```

So, every time an administrator creates a new role and assigns it to a role group, a new role assignment is created. RBAC roles are not similar to security permissions where the most restrictive permission wins. Instead, RBAC will provide additive access to all the roles to a user based on his/her assignment.

Managing exchange certificates

In this section, we will review the use of **Secure Sockets Layer** (**SSL**) certificates in Exchange Organization. SSL is used to secure communications between clients and servers. Clients can be mobile phones, tablets, and computers inside or outside your organization's network. SSL requires you to use digital certificates.

Digital certificates are used for the following purposes:

- **Authentication**: This is used to authenticate the holders of the certificates to be true based on their claims. The holders can be users, websites, and network resources.
- **Encryption**: They are used to protect data that is flowing through the network from tampering and theft.

There are many uses of digital certificates such as web server authentication, **Internet Protocol Security** (**IPSec**), **Transport Layer Security**, **Security/Multipurpose Internet Mail Extensions** (**SMIME**), and for code signing.

Types of Certificates

These are the three types of certificates that we use in Exchange:

- **Self-signed certificates**: A self-signed certificate is a certificate signed by the application that is using it—Exchange in this case. This certificate then establishes *trust* between the Client Access and the Mailbox Server; and hence, they can use it to encrypt and decrypt communication between them. A self-signed certificate is free and provides an easy way to set up Exchange servers for testing/Lab scenarios. Outlook Web App and Exchange ActiveSync protocols work with a self-signed certificate, but Outlook Anywhere requires trusted certificate to be installed and configured. With self-signed certificates, it is difficult to carry out certificate life cycle management activities such as renewal and revocation; so, its use is limited in production Exchange deployments.

- **Windows Public Key Infrastructure certificates**: An infrastructure that is used to manage digital certificates and authenticates claims in electronic transactions is called a **Public Key Infrastructure** (PKI). They consist of certificate authorities who can issue certificates and manage their entire life cycle. In Windows, you can deploy an enterprise certificate authority that integrates with Active Directory, or it can be a standalone certificate authority on a workgroup installation. If you are using certificates issued by an enterprise or a standalone certificate authority, you need to ensure that the trusted root certificate from the certificate authority is located on the trusted root certificate store on each and every device that is trying to connect using SSL to the application.

- **Trusted third-party certificates**: In both self-signed and Windows PKI-based certificates, the device must have the root certificate located in the trusted root certificate store in order for the SSL connection to work. This can be a challenge to distribute the certificates to different devices, especially if you have remote users with multiple devices being used to connect to Exchange servers. In order to solve this problem, there are commercial third-party certificate providers whose root certificates are automatically trusted by the devices. These certificates come at a cost and are usually charged based on the number of names that they support, but they can save a lot of time for administrators planning to distribute root certificate to a range of devices.

In the Exchange server release starting from Exchange 2007 onward, we use certificates for the following services:

- Internet Information Server (IIS):
    - Outlook Web App
    - Exchange Admin Center (EAC)
    - Exchange Web Services
    - Exchange ActiveSync
    - Outlook Anywhere
    - Autodiscover
    - Outlook Address Book distribution
- POP/IMAP
- SMTP

If you look at the default certificates on Exchange Server 2013/2016 post deployment, you will see a self-signed certificate with the Server NetBIOS name and fully qualified domain names in the Subject Alternative Name field, as described previously.

The `Get-ExchangeCertificate` cmdlet will retrieve the properties of all the certificates installed on the Exchange Server under the Personal store in the local computer:

```
Get-ExchangeCertificate | fl
```

If you know the thumbprint of a particular certificate, you can use the `-Thumbprint` parameter as shown in the following screenshot:

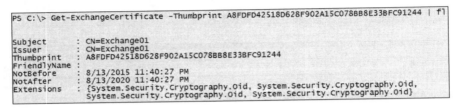

In Exchange Admin Center, you can review the certificate settings under the Servers section in the left navigation pane, and then select the certificates tab as shown in the following screenshot:

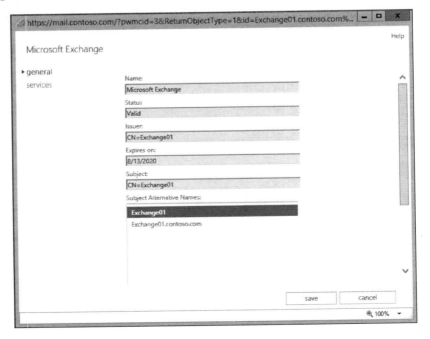

The **services** tab allows you to modify the list of services associated with this certificate as shown in the following screenshot:

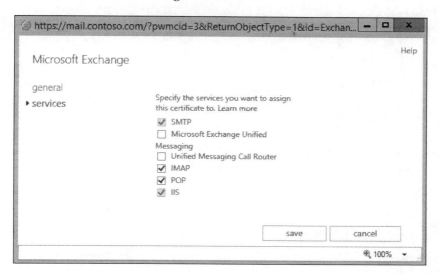

Steps to manage certificates

In the following example, we will review steps for managing certificates on Exchange. The first step is to generate a certificate request from Exchange Management Shell for a certificate with a **Subject Alternative Name (SAN)** and apply this certificate to IIS, POP, IMAP, and SMTP services on Exchange 2013. The command is the same for Exchange 2016 release. Let's see how we do it.

Step 1 – generating a certificate

The first step is to generate a `.csr` file to be submitted to an internal or a third-party certificate authority. For this, the following cmdlet will be used to generate a `.csr` file request for Contoso Corp, and the subject name of the certificate will be `mail.contoso.com`. The subject alternative names will include `contoso.com`, `smtp.contoso.com`, and `autodiscover.contoso.com`:

```
New-ExchangeCertificate -GenerateRequest -SubjectName "c=US, o=Contoso
Corp, cn=mail.contoso.com" -DomainName contoso.com, smtp.contoso.
com, autodiscover.contoso.com -FriendlyName ContosoExchange2013Cert
-RequestFile c:\Exchange2013cert.csr -PrivateKeyExportable $true
```

The resultant `Exchange2013cert.csr` file will be a `base64` encoded file and is enclosed between **-----BEGIN NEW CERTIFICATE REQUEST-----"** and **"-----END NEW CERTIFICATE REQUEST-----** as shown in the following screenshot:

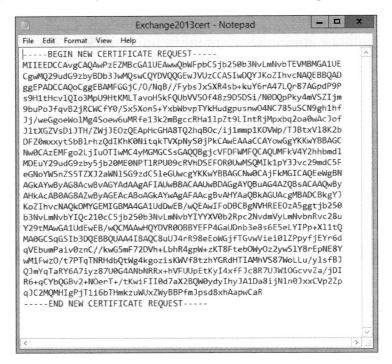

Step 2 – importing the certificate

The second step is to send `Exchange2013cert.csr` file to an internal or a third-party certificate provider. This file will be used to generate certificates. Once the certificate is generated, we will use `Import-ExchangeCertificate` to import the request from the file downloaded from the internal or third=party certificate provider.

The example imports a chain of certificates from `PKCS #7 file Certnew.p7b`:

```
Import-ExchangeCertificate -FileData ([Byte[]]$(Get-Content -Path c:\
Certnew.p7b -Encoding byte -ReadCount 0))
```

```
PS C:\> Import-ExchangeCertificate -FileData ([Byte[]]$(Get-Content -Path c:\Certnew.p7b -Encodi
ng byte -ReadCount 0))

Thumbprint                                Subject
---------                                 -------
43DC0F84057C07528FB35AB62344779DE4D0D506  CN=mail.contoso.com, O=Contoso Corp, C=US
```

The following example imports an existing certificate and private key from the PKCS #12 file called `Certbackup.pfx`:

```
Import-ExchangeCertificate -FileData ([Byte[]]$(Get-Content -Path c:\
Certbackup.pfx -Encoding byte -ReadCount 0)) -Password:(Get-Credential).
password
```

Step 3 – assigning services to the new certificate

The final step is to enable the imported certificate for the Exchange Services such as IIS, POP, IMAP, and SMTP:

```
Enable-ExchangeCertificate -Thumbprint
CE1789ABAEA4A952F224792247EF84686861F5F5 –service IIS,POP,IMAP,SMTP
```

Here is the installed certificate with the subject and the subject alternative name that we have specified in the request:

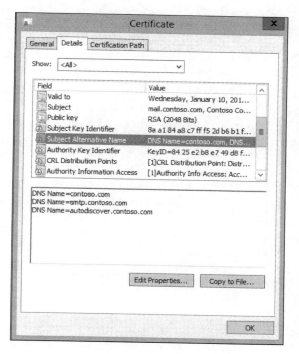

Managing Application Relaying emails

In this section, you will learn how to relay emails through Exchange 2013/2016 servers to internal and external recipients. In Exchange 2013, the Client Access Server role runs a service called Frontend Transport service, which is responsible for email filtering using antispam agents and routing of emails between your Exchange organization and the outside world. The architecture of Exchange 2016 has been further simplified, and it has only the Mailbox server role with required transport services that were earlier handled by the Client Access and Mailbox Roles in Exchange 2013.

There are two additional Transport services hosted by the Mailbox Server roles in Exchange 2013. In Exchange 2016, you will find all these services on the Mailbox Server role:

- **The transport service**: This service is responsible for performing email routing within the Exchange organization such as the Hub Transport server in the previous versions of Exchange. Unlike previous versions, in Exchange 2013/2016, the transport service never talks to the mailbox database, which now has a new service called Mailbox transport service. So, the transport service routes the messages from the Front End transport service, transport service, and the mailbox transport service.

- **The mailbox transport service**: This service is used to exchange messages between the transport service and the mailbox database and is comprised of two separate services: Mailbox Transport Submission and Mailbox Transport Delivery.

In order to set up relay for internal and external recipients, we need to modify the Frontend Transport service, which is a part of the Exchange 2013/2016 Client Access Server role. In Exchange 2013, if you have collocated your Client Access and Mailbox Server on the same hardware or virtual machine, you will still need to configure your Frontend Transport service for relay to work.

All Client Access Servers are configured with a **Default Frontend EXCHANGE01** connector as shown in the following screenshot:

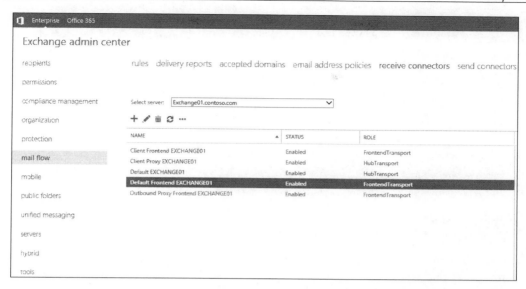

This connector is set up to unauthenticated SMTP connections to allow them to send emails to internal recipients as shown here:

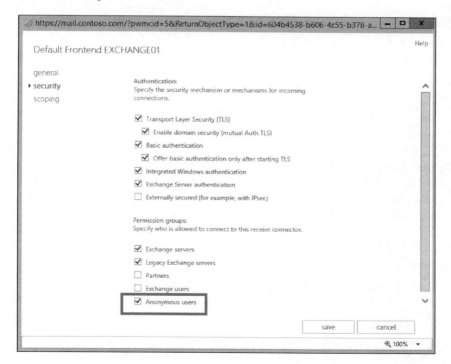

So, if we try to submit a message to one of the internal recipients (administrator in this case) using telnet client, it will be successful. You can see this for yourself in the following screenshot:

```
220 Exchange01.contoso.com Microsoft ESMTP MAIL Service ready at Mon, 7 Sep 2015 18:32:19 +053
helo
250 Exchange01.contoso.com Hello [192.168.10.102]
mail from: test@outlook.com
250 2.1.0 Sender OK
rcpt to: administrator@contoso.com
250 2.1.5 Recipient OK
data
354 Start mail input; end with <CRLF>.<CRLF>
Hello Admin, this is a test email sent from telnet client
.
250 2.6.0 <bd9e9bbb-01ed-4c3c-bd41-b32e0226ee52@Exchange01.contoso.com> [InternalId=9706626089
ntoso.com] Queued mail for delivery
```

If you try to relay through your Exchange 2013/2016 server to one of the external recipients, you will get the "Unable to relay" error.

There are instances when, as an Exchange administrator, you are requested to allow Exchange to relay external recipients. For this to work, we need to create a new Receive connector by typing the following cmdlet.

The following command will create a new receive connector called `Relay-Exchange01` with the transport role set to `FrontendTransport` and the local IP port combination of `192.168.10.102` and `25` and remote IP set to `192.168.10.101`. The `-PermissionsGroups` parameter sets the permission group to well-known security principals in Active directory — Anonymous logon group in this case:

```
New-ReceiveConnector -Name Relay-Exchange01 -Usage Custom -TransportRole
FrontendTransport -Bindings 192.168.10.102:25 -RemoteIPRanges
192.168.10.101 -PermissionGroups AnonymousUsers
```

If you have multiple receive connectors with overlapping `RemoteIPRanges`, then Exchange Server will use the connector with the most specific match. For example, if an inbound SMTP connection is attempted from `192.168.10.100` and `192.168.10.101` IPs, the `Relay-Exchange01` will be used for the `192.168.10.101` connection as it is a specific match and the Default `FrontEnd Exchange01` connector will be used for the other connection.

The next step is to grant `Ms-Exch-SMTP-Accept-Any-Recipient` to the Anonymous Logon group in Active Directory for this receive connector:

```
Get-ReceiveConnector Relay-Exchange01 | Add-ADPermission -User "NT
AUTHORITY\ANONYMOUS LOGON" -ExtendedRights "Ms-Exch-SMTP-Accept-Any-
Recipient"
```

Now, let's run the telnet again and try to relay to an external recipient. This time, the test is successful, which means we have configured relaying through Exchange to external recipients. Yay!

```
220 Exchange01.contoso.com Microsoft ESMTP MAIL Service ready at Mon, 7 Sep 2015 20:29:50 +0530
helo
250 Exchange01.contoso.com Hello [192.168.10.102]
mail from: administrator@contoso.com
250 2.1.0 Sender OK
rcpt to: someone@gmail.com
250 2.1.5 Recipient OK
data
354 Start mail input; end with <CRLF>.<CRLF>
This is an example of relaying to external senders.
.
250 2.6.0 <515b3d93-073f-41b4-bccd-42691694fc0c@Exchange01.contoso.com> [InternalId=97925254349
ntoso.com] Queued mail for delivery
```

Managing External access of Exchange Admin Center

There will be times when you, as an Exchange administrator, may want to restrict the use of Exchange Admin Center (EAC) for External users for security reasons.

If you disable EAC access on Exchange 2013/2016 Client access servers, it will be disabled for all internal and external users. If you need access to EAC for internal use only, you have to deploy a separate Client Access Server role and configure it to handle internal requests only through the following cmdlet:

```
Set-ECPVirtualDirectory -Identity "Exchange01\ecp (default web site)"
-AdminEnabled $True
```

The following command will turn off EAC access for all users on server Exchange01:

```
Set-ECPVirtualDirectory -Identity "Exchange01\ecp (default web site)"
-AdminEnabled $False
```

Writing a basic script

Let's take an example from http://blogs.technet.com/b/heyscriptingguy/archive/2011/02/16/use-powershell-and-net-to-find-expired-certificates.aspx and write a simple script that will check the certificate expiry on the Local Machine certificate store and list the Issue, Subject, Thumbprint, and expiry date. The .NET class called System.Security.Cryptography.X509Certificates.X509Store is used for this script.

The following code will connect to the certificate store:

```
$Certstore = New-Object System.Security.Cryptography.X509Certificates.
X509Store("My","LocalMachine")

$Certstore.Open("ReadWrite")

$Certstore.Certificates
```

Here, we will use a variable called $certstore to use a new object with the X509 class to call two values, the location of the store and the name of the store. The second line of the code opens the store in the read write mode. The following table lists the name of the X509 certificate store to open:

Member name	Description
Address Book	The X.509 certificate store for other users
Auth Root	The X.509 certificate store for third-party certificate authorities (CAs)
Certificate Authority	The X.509 certificate store for intermediate certificate authorities (CAs)
Disallowed	The X.509 certificate store for revoked certificates
My	The X.509 certificate store for personal certificates
Root	The X.509 certificate store for trusted root certificate authorities (CAs)
Trusted People	The X.509 certificate store for directly trusted people and resources
Trusted Publisher	The X.509 certificate store for directly trusted publishers

Source of the above table data is:

https://msdn.microsoft.com/en-us/library/system.security.
cryptography.x509certificates.storename(v=vs.110).aspx.

The script will list the Issuer, Thumbprint, Subject name, and expiry date on a particular server where it is executed. We can modify this to include remote servers and add a section to send an email to the administrators. Then, we will schedule the script using a schedule task to get updates 45 days (in this case) before the certificate expiry on our Exchange servers:

```
$daysremaining = 45

$Expiry = (Get-Date).AddDays($daysremaining)

$Certstore=new-object System.Security.Cryptography.X509Certificates.
X509Store("\\Exchange01\my","LocalMachine")

$Certstore.open("ReadWrite")

$certstore.certificates | Foreach-object {

If ($_.NotAfter -lt $Expiry) {$_ | Select Issuer, Thumbprint, Subject,
NotAfter | Format-List}

}
```

Summary

In this chapter, you have learned how to delegate Exchange administration using RBAC, Manage certificates, and relaying of emails. We also configured the ECP virtual directory to toggle access for administrators from the external and internal network.

In the next chapter, we will cover how to manage address book, email address, and Retention Policies in Exchange 2013 and 2016.

5
Everything about Microsoft Exchange Policies

In this chapter, we will cover the management of proxy addresses of recipients through E-mail Address Policies. Next segmentation of Global Address List will be covered through the use of Address book policies. We will finish this chapter by covering the messaging records management that manages the entire e-mail life cycle and reduces legal/compliance risks using Retention Policies and Tags.

The following topics will be covered in this chapter:

- Introducing Exchange Policies
- Creating and managing E-mail Address Policies
- Creating and managing Address book policies
- Creating and managing Retention Policies
- Automating Retention Policies
- Writing a basic script

Introducing Exchange Policies

You will learn about E-Mail Address Policies, the address book, and retention in this chapter.

In order to generate primary and secondary E-Mail addresses for recipients, which include users, groups, contacts, and resources, we use E-Mail Address Policies in an Exchange organization.

The next topic covers address book policies introduced in Exchange 2010 and is available in the Exchange 2013 and 2016 versions. Prior to the introduction of address book policies, the segmentation of Address Lists within an Exchange organization was a complicated process of managing Active Directory Access Control Lists to allow and deny access and using Query-based DN for directory searches.

Finally, we will end this chapter by reviewing how the e-mail lifecycle can be managed by the messaging records management. As an administrator, you will be able to define when an e-mail moves from a user's primary mailbox to archive or whether it is to be deleted permanently once it reaches the retention age.

Creating and managing E-mail Address Policies

We will first take a look at accepted domains and then come back to E-Mail Address Policies. An accepted domain is an SMTP name for which the Exchange organization is responsible for sending and receiving E-Mails.

There are three types of accepted domains:

- **Authoritative:** This is the domain with recipient's mailboxes hosted in your Exchange organization. If a domain is set to authoritative and the recipient is not found in Active Directory, a **Non-Delivery Report** (**NDR**) is sent to the sender.

- **Internal relay**: In this scenario, the domain will not have all the recipient's mailboxes in your Exchange organization. For example, you have Exchange and Lotus Domino as your messaging environment and a SMTP domain is shared between these two. In this case, you will configure the SMTP domain as internal relay and create a send connector for this domain that points to Lotus Domino where the rest of the mailboxes are located. If a recipient is not found in Active Directory, Exchange will look for a send connector with the closest match of the SMTP address space and route the e-mail to the other messaging environment.

- **External relay**: The difference between internal and external relay is based on the location of two messaging infrastructure. Internal relay is for scenarios where both the messaging infrastructures are inside your network boundary. External relay is for scenarios where the other messaging system is beyond your organization's network. For example, if you want to share a SMTP namespace with another company or an independent business unit, you will configure it as an external relay domain.

The default accepted domain that is listed in Exchange will be your Active Directory namespace. You need to add additional accepted domains with different types based on your scenario before you can use them in your E-mail Address Policies. For example, if you want to use `contoso.com` and all its child domains, you need to use `*.contoso.com` as your SMTP namespace.

The e-mail address stamped by the default E-Mail address policy will have the format of `alias@defaultaccepteddomain.com`. The alias that appears before the 'at sign' (@) is called the local part of the E-mail Address. This local part of the E-mail Address can be modified based on the following variables:

Variable	Value
%g	Given name (first name)
%i	Middle initial
%s	Surname (last name)
%d	Display name
%m	Exchange alias
%xs	Uses the first x letters of the surname. For example, if x = 2, the first two letters of the surname are used
%xg	Uses the first x letters of the given name. For example, if x = 2, the first two letters of the given name are used

Source of the content—`https://technet.microsoft.com/en-us/library/bb232171(v=exchg.150).aspx`.

So, if you want your users to use `firstname.lastname@defaultaccepteddomain.com`, you will use the `%g.%s@defaultaccepteddomain.com` variable in your E-mail address policy.

At times, you need to work with non-SMTP e-mail address if you are working with Lotus or Novell GroupWise coexistence with Exchange environments. Exchange supports the following non-SMTP e-mail address formats:

- EX (Legacy DN Proxy Address Prefix Display Name)
- X.500
- X.400
- MSMail
- CcMail
- Lotus Notes

- Novell GroupWise
- Exchange Unified Messaging proxy address (EUM proxy address)

All the non-SMTP address types are considered custom types and Exchange will not provide the wizard and property pages for X400, Lotus Domino, or GroupWise address types. So, if you are using any of these address types, you must have the dynamic link library (DLL) file used for these address generators. If you don't have the file, these custom addresses will not be stamped on recipients, and you will get an error message indicating that the DLL file is missing.

Now, let's go ahead and create a new E-Mail Address Policy that will stamp the first four letters of the first name with the last name for a new authoritative accepted domain called `fabricam.com`.

The first step is to add `*.fabrikam.com` as the accepted domain, which can be achieved by typing the following cmdlet in Exchange Management Shell. We used a wildcard character as we are going to use one of the subdomains in the later example while creating a new E-Mail Address Policy:

```
New-AcceptedDomain -DomainName *.fabrikam.com -DomainType Authoritative
-Name Fabrikam
```

You can configure accepted domains through Exchange Admin Center by navigating to the **Mail Flow | accepted domain** tab as shown in the following screenshot:

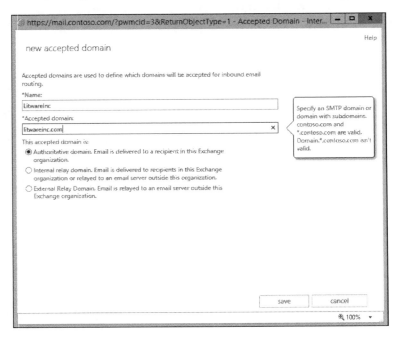

Now, we will create an E-Mail Address policy that will include all the mailbox users whose departments have the value Tax, Controller, and more, and it will stamp the primary e-mail address of their given name followed by the first two letters of the surname and then @finance.fabrikam.com:

```
New-EmailAddressPolicy -Name "Finance Users" -IncludedRecipients
MailboxUsers -ConditionalDepartment "Controller","Accounts
Payable","Accounts Receivable","Payroll","Treasury","Tax"
-EnabledEmailAddressTemplates "SMTP:%g%2s@finance.fabrikam.com"
```

You can review the settings through Exchange Admin Center (EAC) by navigating to the **Mail Flow | email address**.

In order to test the previous policy on one of the existing mailboxes, change the department attribute to Tax, Payroll, or any of those listed in the previous command. Then, run the following cmdlet:

```
Update-EmailAddressPolicy -Identity "Finance Users"
```

Now, check the e-mail address of the mailbox. It should have the primary e-mail address as follows:

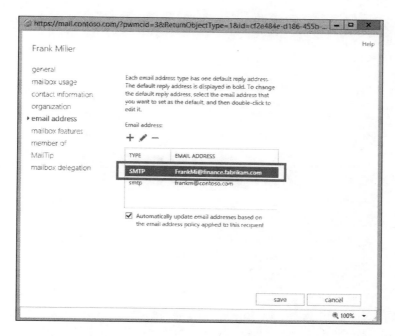

In the next section, you will learn how to use address book policies for the segmentation of address books within a single Exchange organization.

Creating and managing Address Book policies

In Exchange 2010 SP2, Address Book Policies were introduced to help administrators segregate the address lists between different departments or business units within a single Exchange organization. There was a whitepaper on how to segregate address lists using Exchange 2007, but it was complicated, and there was limited support while upgrading to Exchange 2010 SP2 or the **Hosted Messaging and Collaboration (HMC)** platforms, which were primarily used by commercial e-mail hosters to host multiple customers on a single exchange organization, creating a logical isolation between the customer's organizations.

Address Book Policies (ABPs) contain the following:

- One or more address lists
- One default address list
- One room address list
- One offline address book

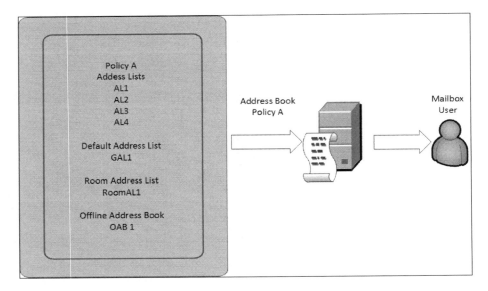

You can create multiple **Address Book Policies** (ABPs) such as the one in the picture and assign it to mailbox users. They take effect when the user's application tries to connect to e-mail address book service on the Client Access Server role.

ABPs allow us to logically separate one Exchange organization to multiple independent units where users in one department will not be able to view other users from other departments or business units in any of the address lists. Here are some of the best practices we need to follow when deploying ABPs:

- The user mailboxes should be hosted on Exchange 2010 SP2 and later versions.

- Client Access server roles should not be deployed on Active Directory global catalog servers. If you run Client Access servers on global catalog servers, the **Name Service Provider Interface (NSPI)** will be used for the address book query instead of the Exchange address book service and ABPs created will be ineffective.

- The Room list is a must for all ABPs. If you are not using Room lists, you can create an empty one and associate it with the ABPs.

- Hierarchical address books (HABs) and ABPs do not work simultaneously. It will be one or the other.

- Clients such as Entourage or Outlook for Mac use LDAP queries when internal to the network; they will connect to the Domain controllers and ABPs will not work for them. If you have these clients in your network, plan your network access in such a way that these clients connect to Exchange from an external network. In this case, they will use Exchange web services and ABPs will apply to them.

- Deploying ABPs alone will not restrict users from sending e-mails to users in another virtual organization. If you want to prevent users from sending e-mails to other virtual organizations, you have to use transport rules to restrict the e-mail flow.

- The Global Address list must contain all the address lists including the Room list.

- Distribution groups should not span across different departments when using ABPs, otherwise you will run into the following issues:

    ○ If someone sends an e-mail to a group with a read or delivery receipt, and the group contains members from other department or virtual organizations, the sender will be able to see the members in the other organization.

    ○ The Get-Group cmdlets will not be impacted by ABPs. It means if you have a distribution group with members from two virtual organizations and you execute the Get-Group cmdlet, it will list all the users of the group based on the permission of the user who is executing the cmdlet.

Now, let's configure ABPs for the following scenario. LitwareInc have acquired another company called ProsewareInc. Each of these organizations uses Exchange 2010 SP2 or later versions and has already migrated mailboxes from ProsewareInc to the LitwareInc Exchange organization. They want to run operations as separate business units with no common management hierarchy and shared employees.

Now, with this information, we will deploy ABPs for these two companies in our Exchange organization. Here are the steps to deploy ABPs:

First, begin with the installation and configuration of address book policy routing agents.

We are going to install the ABPs transport agent by running the following command:

```
Install-Transport Agent -Name "ABP Routing Agent" -
TransportAgentFactory "Microsoft.Exchange.Transport.Agent.
AddressBookPolicyRoutingAgent.AddressBookPolicyRoutingAgentFactory"
-AssemblyPath $env:ExchangeInstallPath\TransportRoles\agents\
AddressBookPolicyRoutingAgent\Microsoft.Exchange.Transport.Agent.
AddressBookPolicyRoutingAgent.dll
```

The next step is to enable the ABPs routing agent:

```
Enable-TransportAgent "ABP Routing Agent"
```

Restart the transport service after enabling the agent and verify the installation by running the following commands:

```
Restart-Service MSExchangeTransport
```

```
Get-TransportAgent
```

The following command enables the ABPs routing agent:

```
Set-TransportConfig -AddressBookPolicyRoutingEnabled $true
```

The next step is to divide the Exchange organization using the customattribute 1-15 properties instead of attributes such as Company, StateorProvince, or Department as these attributes are not available for all recipient types. For example, the attributes such as Company, Department, and so on are not available for cmdlets for mail-enabled users, contacts, and distribution groups.

So, we will create two organizational units called LitwareInc and ProsewareInc and use CustomAttribute5 for our users, contacts, and distribution groups. We will then use the LitwareInc and ProsewareInc values as values for the respective Organization Units.

Here are the commands that you can use once you have created the mailboxes, contacts, and distribution groups in the respective Organizational Units to populate CustomAttribute5:

For user mailboxes, perform the following:

```
Get-Mailbox -OrganizationalUnit LitwareInc | Set-Mailbox CustomAttribute5
"LitwareInc"
```

```
Get-Mailbox -OrganizationalUnit  ProsewareInc| Set-Mailbox
CustomAttribute5 " ProsewareInc"
```

For Distribution groups, perform the following:

```
Get-DistributionGroup-OrganizationalUnit LitwareInc| Set-
DistributionGroup CustomAttribute5 "LitwareInc "
```

```
Get-DistributionGroup-OrganizationalUnit ProsewareInc | Set-
DistributionGroup CustomAttribute5 "ProsewareInc"
```

For contacts, perform the following:

```
Get-MailContact -OrganizationalUnit LitwareInc | Set-MailContact -
CustomAttribute5 "LitwareInc"
```

```
Get-MailContact -OrganizationalUnit ProsewareInc | Set-MailContact -
CustomAttribute5 " ProsewareInc"
```

So, we will create two ABPs for LitwareInc and ProsewareInc with their own address lists, room lists, Global Address list, and Offline address books with a recipient filter of CustomAttribute5. Here is the list of objects that need to be created:

Litware Inc	Proseware Inc
Users and Distribution groups All_Litwareinc_Users_DG All_Litwareinc_Groups	Users and Distribution groups All_Prosewareinc_Users_DG All_Prosewareinc_Groups
Conference Rooms – Room List All_Litwareinc_Rooms	Conference Rooms – Room List All_Prosewareinc_Rooms
Contacts: All_Litwareinc_Contacts	Contacts: All_Prosewareinc_Contacts
Global Address List: GAL_Litwareinc	Global Address List: GAL_Prosewareinc
Offline Address Book : OAB_Litwareinc	Offline Address Book : OAB_Prosewareinc

In the next step, we are going to create the address lists in line with the following table:

Objects	LitwareInc	ProsewareInc
Address Lists	AL_LiwareInc_Groups	AL_ProsewareInc_Groups
	AL_LiwareInc_Users	AL_ProsewareInc_Users
	AL_LiwareInc_Contacts	AL_ProsewareInc_Contacts
Global address lists	GAL_LiwareInc	GAL_ProsewareInc
Room address lists	AL_LiwareInc_Rooms	AL_ProsewareInc_Rooms
Offline address books (OAB)	OAB_LiwareInc	OAB_ProsewareInc

The command will create address lists for Mailboxes and distribution groups for LitwareInc and ProsewareInc:

```
New-AddressList -Name "AL_LiwareInc_Users_DG" -RecipientFilter
{((RecipientType -eq 'UserMailbox') -or (RecipientType -eq
"MailUniversalDistributionGroup") -or (RecipientType -eq
"DynamicDistributionGroup")) -and (CustomAttribute5 -eq "LiwareInc")}
```

```
New-AddressList -Name "AL_ProsewareInc_Users_DG" -RecipientFilter
{((RecipientType -eq 'UserMailbox') -or (RecipientType -eq
"MailUniversalDistributionGroup") -or (RecipientType -eq
"DynamicDistributionGroup")) -and (CustomAttribute5 -eq "ProsewareInc")}
```

The following command will create address lists for contacts for both the organizations:

```
New-AddressList -Name "AL_LiwareInc_Contacts" -RecipientFilter
{(RecipientType -eq 'MailContact') -and (CustomAttribute5 -eq
"LiwareInc")}
```

```
New-AddressList -Name "AL_ProsewareInc_Contacts" -RecipientFilter
{(RecipientType -eq 'MailContact') -and (CustomAttribute5 -eq
"ProsewareInc")}
```

This is for the room list of LiwareInc and ProsewareInc:

```
New-AddressList -Name AL_LiwareInc_Rooms -RecipientFilter {(Alias -ne
$null) -and (CustomAttribute5 -eq "LiwareInc")-and (RecipientDisplayType
-eq 'ConferenceRoomMailbox') -or (RecipientDisplayType -eq
'SyncedConferenceRoomMailbox')}
```

```
New-AddressList -Name AL_ProsewareInc_Rooms -RecipientFilter
{(Alias -ne $null) -and (CustomAttribute5 -eq "ProsewareInc")-
and (RecipientDisplayType -eq 'ConferenceRoomMailbox') -or
(RecipientDisplayType -eq 'SyncedConferenceRoomMailbox')}
```

Now, we have to create Global Address Lists:

```
New-GlobalAddressList -Name "GAL_LiwareInc" -RecipientFilter
{(CustomAttribute5 -eq "LiwareInc")}
```

```
New-GlobalAddressList -Name "GAL_ProsewareInc" -RecipientFilter
{(CustomAttribute5 -eq "ProsewareInc")}
```

Finally, we create the Offline Address Book:

```
New-OfflineAddressBook -Name "OAB_LiwareInc" -AddressLists "GAL_
LiwareInc"
```

```
New-OfflineAddressBook -Name "OAB_ProsewareInc" -AddressLists "GAL_
ProsewareInc"
```

Next, we are going to create new ABPs for LiwareInc and ProsewareInc users and assign these policies to the users:

```
New-AddressBookPolicy -Name "ABP_LiwareInc" -AddressLists "AL_LiwareInc_
Users_DG","AL_LiwareInc_Contacts" -OfflineAddressBook "\OAB_LiwareInc"
-GlobalAddressList "\GAL_LiwareInc" -RoomList "\AL_LiwareInc_Rooms"
```

```
New-AddressBookPolicy -Name "ABP_ProsewareInc" -AddressLists "AL_
ProsewareInc_Users_DG","AL_ProsewareInc_Contacts" -OfflineAddressBook "\
OAB_ProsewareInc" -GlobalAddressList "\GAL_ProsewareInc" -RoomList "\
AL_ProsewareInc_Rooms"
```

The following command will apply the new ABPs to the mailboxes on LiwareInc and ProsewareInc OUs whose CustomAttribute5 has been populated earlier in Step 2:

```
Get-Mailbox -resultsize unlimited | where {$_.CustomAttribute5 -eq
"LiwareInc"} | Set-Mailbox -AddressBookPolicy "ABP_LiwareInc"
```

```
Get-Mailbox -resultsize unlimited | where {$_.CustomAttribute5 -eq
"ProsewareInc"} | Set-Mailbox -AddressBookPolicy "ABP_ProsewareInc"
```

Now is the time to test the ABP configuration. Try logging in with a user who is located in LiwareInc Organizational Unit, and create an outlook profile, and try to find users in ProsewareIncusers. The ABPs will not allow users in LiwareInc or ProsewareInc Organizational Units to view the GAL of other department or virtual organization.

Creating and managing Retention Policies

Messaging Records Management (MRM) is used in Exchange 2010 and later versions to manage the e-mail lifecycle based on business, legal, and compliance requirements and for efficient storage management. Starting with Exchange 2010, retention tags and policies are introduced for MRM. Once you create a retention tag, you can apply it to an entire mailbox and default mailbox folders such as Inbox and Sent Items. You can also create personal tags that allow your users to apply them to individual items or folders using Outlook or Outlook Web App. Once the retention age is reached for a particular item, Managed Folder Assistant, which runs on mailbox servers, takes the action specified in the tag. For example, it can move the item to the Users In-Place archive or delete the message permanently.

Let's understand the different types of retention tags available and how they can be linked in a retention policy and applied to user mailboxes.

Retention tags can be of three types based on where they can be applied and who can use them:

- **Default Policy Tag (DPT)**: This tag is configured by administrator and meant for all untagged items in the mailbox, which doesn't have a retention tag applied. The users will not be able to change these tags. The actions available to DPTs are Move to archive, Delete and Allow recovery, and Permanently Delete.

- **Retention Policy Tag (RPT)**: These tags are also configured by the administrator and applied automatically to the default folders such as Inbox, Sent, and Deleted Items. End users cannot make changes to RPT applied to default folders. The actions that you can use with RPTs are Delete and Allow Recovery, and Permanently Delete.

- **Personal Tag:** Personal tags are used by end users to tag items either through inbox rules or manually using Outlook or Outlook Web App. The actions available to Personal tags are Move to archive, Delete and allow recovery, and Permanently Delete.

Now that you have learned the different types of retention tags, let's understand the use of Retention Policies that group these tags based on retention, business, and legal requirements.

A retention policy can have the following:

- One **Default Policy Tag** (**DPT**) for Moving items to Archive action
- One Default Policy Tag (DPT) for Deleting and Allowing recovery or Permanently Delete actions
- One Default Policy Tag (DPT) for voice mail messages with Delete and allow recovery or Permanently Delete action
- One Retention Policy Tag (RPT) for each default folder
- Any number of personal tags

Now, let's configure retention tags and policies for Contoso. Here are the retention requirements:

- Items from all the Default folders should be moved to archive after 90 days
- Items in the Deleted Items folder should be permanently deleted after 365 days (1 year)
- Users should have the option to retain items for up to 1,825 days (5 years)

In order to meet the previous requirements, we need to create a Default Policy Tag (DPT), which will move items from Users Primary Mailbox to his Archive Mailbox after 90 days. Next, we will create a Retention Policy tag for Deleted Items that will permanently delete items after 365 days. For the last requirement, we need to create a personal tag 1825 as the retention age that users can use to tag items, which should be retained for 5 years.

The following command will create a Default Policy Tag to move items to archive after 90 days. Note that we have used the—Type All parameter for DPTs:

```
New-RetentionPolicyTag "90 Days Archive" -Type All -Comment "This tag
moves all items to archive after 90 days" -RetentionEnabled $true
-AgeLimitForRetention 90 -RetentionAction MoveToArchive
```

For the next requirement, we will use a Retention Policy Tag (RPT) on DeletedItems, which will permanently delete items after 1 year:

```
New-RetentionPolicyTag "Deleted Items Cleanup - 1 year" -Type
DeletedItems -Comment "This tag permanently deletes e-mail from
the Deleted Items folder after 1 year" -RetentionEnabled $true
-AgeLimitForRetention 365 -RetentionAction PermanentlyDelete
```

The last requirement is to create a Personal tag that will allow users to tag items for up to 5 years before deleting them:

```
New-RetentionPolicyTag "Business Critical - 5 years retention" -Type
Personal -Comment "This tag must be used for all business critical mails"
-RetentionEnabled $true -AgeLimitForRetention 1825 -RetentionAction
PermanentlyDelete
```

The next step is to create a Retention Policy with all these tags in it and then apply it to the user's mailbox:

```
New-RetentionPolicy "Contoso General Retention Policy"
-RetentionPolicyTagLinks "90 Days Archive","Deleted Items Cleanup - 1
year","Business Critical - 5 years retention"
```

The following command will apply this policy to Amy Albert's mailbox. You can use the output of the `Get-Mailbox` cmdlet with a filter and pipe the output objects to the `Set-Mailbox` cmdlet to assign this to all or a specific group of users in your Exchange organization:

```
Set-Mailbox -Identity "Amy Alberts" -RetentionPolicy "Contoso General
Retention Policy"
```

```
Get-Mailbox -ResultSize Unlimited | Set-Mailbox -RetentionPolicy "Contoso
General Retention Policy"
```

If you want to start the processing of messages immediately for all mailboxes, you need to use the `Start-ManagedFolderAssistant` cmdlet:

```
Get-Mailbox -Filter {(RecipientTypeDetails -eq 'UserMailbox')} | ForEach
{Start-ManagedFolderAssistant $_.Identity}
```

Writing a basic script

There are times when, as an administrator, you need secondary SMTP addresses to be added to mailboxes.

You can use a .csv file to list all the users with their alias and new e-mail addresses in the following format and save it as the `E-mailAddresses.csv` file:

```
alias,e-mailaddress
hollyh,hollyh@wingtiptoys.com
amya,amya@wingtiptoys.com
susanb,susanb@wingtiptoys.com
```

Then, use the following command either directly on Exchange Management Shell or save it in a `.PS1` file:

```
Import-Csv c:\Scripts\E-mailaddresses.csv | Foreach{set-mailbox -identity
$_.Alias -E-mailAddresses @{add=$_.e-mailaddress}}
```

Summary

In this chapter, you learned all about managing E-Mail Address Policies. Then, we reviewed how to segregate address lists using Address Book Policies. Finally, we saw e-mail lifecycle management using Messaging Records Management (MRM) and Retention Policies in Exchange 2013 and Exchange online.

In the next chapter, we will discuss configuring Exchange Client Access and Transport Services.

6

Handling Exchange Server Roles

Five different server roles were introduced with the release of Exchange 2007 and 2010. These were Mailbox, Client Access, Hub Transport, Edge Transport, and Unified messaging role. They were introduced to optimize the use of system resources that were available at that time. Later, this was reduced to just Mailbox, Client Access, and Edge Transport in Exchange 2013. With the release of Exchange 2016, we just have two roles: Mailbox and Edge Transport.

In this chapter, we will configure the Client Access Services, such as POP, IMAP, Outlook Anywhere, and ActiveSync and different transport components. At the end, we will review the usage and configuration of Public folder mailboxes as a part of the Mailbox server role.

The following topics will be covered in this chapter:

- Configuring POP, IMAP, ActiveSync, and Outlook anywhere
- Managing Client Access Servers
- Managing Transport connectors
- Managing DSN Messages
- Managing Message Tracking logs
- Managing Transport Queues
- Managing Public Folder Mailboxes
- Writing a basic script

Configuring POP, IMAP, ActiveSync, and Outlook Anywhere

If you are managing an Exchange organization in a heterogeneous environment where you have all kinds of clients connecting to Exchange, the chances are that you have your POP3 and IMAP4 services enabled in your Exchange Client Access Servers.

Let's see the usage of POP3 and IMAP4 protocols in Exchange

Configuring POP3 and IMAP4POP3 is a widely used protocol for e-mail access. The POP3 client downloads the messages to a client computer, and then these messages are removed from the server. However, there are a few POP3 applications that allow you to keep a copy of the message on your server so that it can be accessed from a different device. POP3 allows e-mails to be downloaded to one folder (inbox) in client computers, and it doesn't have the capability to synchronize multiple folders.

IMAP4 offers more features than POP3 such as support for a copy of e-mail messages kept on the server to be accessed from a different location. It allows creating multiple folders on the server. Some IMAP4 applications also allow downloading only the header of the e-mail messages stored on the server. Using this, users can only download the messages that they want to read and leave the rest on the server.

Both POP3 and IMAP4 protocols do not support collaboration features such as calendaring, contacts, and task management. Both POP3 and IMAP4 email clients use SMTP to send messages.

There are lots of client applications that support POP3 and IMAP4 protocols including Outlook, Windows Live Mail, Outlook Express, Entourage, Mozilla Thunderbird, Eudora, and more. Features supported by each of these email applications may vary, and you need to review the documentation of these client applications for feature details.

By default, POP3 and IMAP4 is disabled in Exchange 2013/2016. So, the first step is to enable POP3 and IMAP4 on Client Access and the Mailbox server role using the following commands in Exchange 2013. As there is only a single mailbox server role in Exchange 2016, you need to execute the commands on the mailbox server role in 2016 release.

On the Client Access Server, the following commands will set the service startup to automatic and start the service:

```
Set-service msExchangePOP3 -startuptype automatic
Start-service msExchangePOP3
```

This will set the POP3 Backend Service startup type and start the service on the Mailbox Server role:

```
Set-service msExchangePOP3BE -startuptype automatic
Start-service msExchangePOP3BE
```

Similarly, to enable IMAP4 on Client Access Server, execute the following:

```
Set-service msExchangeIMAP4 -startuptype automatic
Start-service msExchangeIMAP4
```

Similarly, to enable IMAP4 on the Mailbox server, execute the following:

```
Set-service msExchangeIMAP4BE -startuptype automatic
Start-service msExchangeIMAP4BE
```

After enabling the services, the next step is to provide information to your users so that they can configure their e-mail clients to connect to Exchange using POP3, IMAP4, and the SMTP protocol. These settings include the POP3 and IMAP4 server names, the Port number, and the encryption method.

By default, if users log into their Outlook Web App Settings / Options / Account / My account / Settings for the POP or IMAP access, it will not display any configuration settings. These settings can be populated by the use of the Set-POPSettings, Set-IMAPSettings, and Set-ReceiveConnector cmdlets.

The following command will set the hostname, port number, and encryption settings for the POP3 and IMAP4 services on server Exchange01:

```
Set-PopSettings -ExternalConnectionSetting {Exchange01.Contoso.
com:995:SSL}
Set-IMAPSettings -ExternalConnectionSetting {Exchange01.Contoso.
com:993:SSL}
```

Internet Information Server (IIS) needs to be restarted after executing the previous commands. The following command will advertise the SMTP settings through the OWA Options page:

```
Set-ReceiveConnector "Client Frontend Exchange01"
-AdvertiseClientSettings $True -FQDN Exchange01.Contoso.com
```

Now, if users log into their Outlook Web App `Settings` / `Options` / `Account` / `My account` / `Settings` for the POP or IMAP access, they will get the settings required to configure POP3 and IMAP4 clients, as shown here:

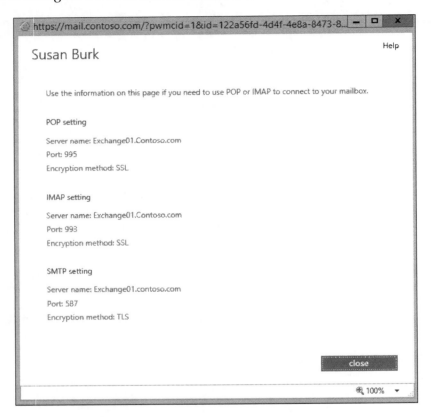

Configuring ActiveSync

Exchange ActiveSync (EAS) is a communication protocol optimized to work with low-bandwidth and high-latency networks. This protocol is used to synchronize e-mails, calendar, contacts, tasks, and notes from the Exchange server mailbox and your mobile device. This protocol is based on XML and uses HTTP and HTTPS for communication. By default, EAS is enabled for all users on an Exchange server and allows users to synchronize their mobile devices.

Let's first check the status of Exchange ActiveSync Features for a user named Holly Holt:

```
Get-CASMailbox -Identity "Holly Holt" | FL ActiveSyncEnabled
```

If you want to disable it for Susan Burk, use this command:

```
Set-CASMailbox -Identity "Susan Burk" -ActiveSyncEnabled $False
```

The following command enables ActiveSync for all your users:

```
Get-Mailbox -ResultSize Unlimited | Set-CASMailbox -ActiveSyncEnabled
$True
```

Now, let's look at how to configure and modify the existing ActiveSyncMailbox Policies. You can specify the parameters while you create the policy using New-ActiveSyncMailboxPolicy. Or, you can do so later using the Set-ActiveSyncMailboxPolicy cmdlet. You can always review the help with these cmdlets using the Get-Help cmdlet:

```
New-ActiveSyncMailboxPolicy -Name:"Contoso_All_Users_Policy"
-DevicePasswordEnabled:$true -AlphanumericDevicePasswordReq
uired:$true -PasswordRecoveryEnabled:$true -IsDefault:$false
-AttachmentsEnabled:$false -AllowStorageCard:$False

New-ActiveSyncMailboxPolicy -Name:"Management_Users_Policy"
-AllowBluetooth:Allow -AllowBrowser:$true -AllowCamera:$true
-AllowPOPIMAPEmail:$false -DevicePasswordEnabled:$true -Alphanu
mericDevicePasswordRequired:$true -PasswordRecoveryEnabled:$true
-MaxEmailAgeFilter:TwoWeeks -AllowWiFi:$true -AllowStorageCard:$true
```

You can use the Get-ActiveSyncMailboxPolicy cmdlet to view the settings of an existing policy:

```
Get-ActiveSyncMailboxPolicy -Identity "Management_Users_Policy"
```

Use the Set-AciveSyncMailboxPolicy cmdlet to modify the settings:

```
Set-ActiveSyncMailboxPolicy -Identity:"Management_Users_Policy"
-DevicePasswordEnabled:$true -AlphanumericDevicePasswordRequired
:$False -PasswordRecoveryEnabled:$true -AttachmentsEnabled:$true
-MaxInactivityTimeDeviceLock:00:15:00 -IsDefault:$false
```

One of the other features of EAS is the ability to use remote wipe for lost or stolen devices. You can initiate a remote wipe through Exchange Admin Center, Exchange Management Shell, or Outlook Web App.

In order to do a remote wipe using Shell, we need to find the device name associated with the mailbox of Holly Holt using either of these commands:

```
Get-MobileDevice -Identity "hollyh"
```

```
Get-MobileDevice -Identity "Contoso\hollyh"
```

Next, use the following command to wipe the device named WM_HollyHolt, which we got from the earlier command, and send a notification to the administrator@contoso.com e-mail address:

```
Clear-MobileDevice -Identity WM_HollyHolt -NotificationEmailAddresses
administrator@contoso.com
```

Get-ActiveSyncDeviceStatistics is used to get the statistics of a mobile device configured with an Exchange 2013 or Exchange online mailbox.

The following command will display the statistics of mobile devices associated with the mailbox of Amy Alberts (amya). As per Microsoft Exchange Documentation in TechNet https://technet.microsoft.com/en-us/library/aa996908(v=exchg.160).aspx, the cmdlet called Get-ActiveSyncDeviceStatistics will be removed from the future Exchange versions, so it is safe to use Get-MobileDeviceStatistics instead:

```
Get-ActiveSyncDeviceStatistics -Identity Amya

Get-MobileDeviceStatistics -Identity HollyH
```

You can also use this command to send the Exchange ActiveSync log file to the Helpdesk e-mail address:

```
Get-MobileDeviceStatistics -Mailbox Amya -GetMailboxLog $true
-NotificationEmailAddresses ITSupport@contoso.com
```

Next, we will consider an example to use the Exchange ActiveSync device access rule to block or allow access. With Exchange 2010, the Allow/Block/Quarantine list is released as a feature and is now available in Exchange 2013 and 2016 and Exchange Online. This helps organizations to control which of the ActiveSync enabled devices or device families are allowed, blocked, or quarantined as they connect to Exchange servers.

This can be accessed through Exchange Admin Center by navigating to **Mobile | Mobile Device Access** as shown in the following screenshot:

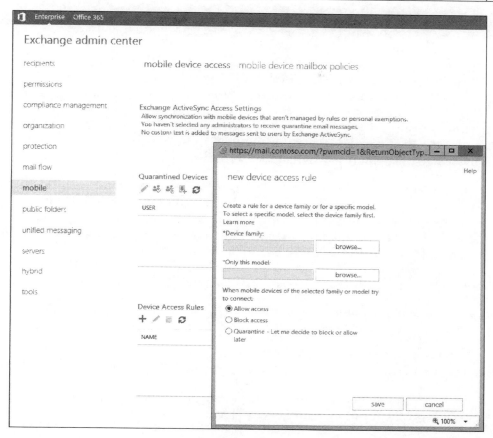

If you would like to use Shell to restrict or allow access, the first step is to list all the properties of mobile devices in your organization:

```
Get-MobileDevice | Format-List DeviceOS,DeviceModel,DeviceType
```

Then, we will use the following command to block access for iPhones:

```
New-ActiveSyncDeviceAccessRule -AccessLevel Block -Characteristic
DeviceModel -QueryString iPhone
```

Configuring Outlook Anywhere

Outlook Anywhere uses the Windows RPC over the HTTP Proxy component to wrap the remote procedure calls (RPCs) within an HTTP layer. This ensures that the network traffic, which is HTTP/HTTPs in this case, traverses through firewalls without requiring a large number of RPC ports to be opened. By default, Exchange 2013/2016 enables Outlook Anywhere, and it doesn't allow a direct RPC connectivity. You need to configure a valid SSL certificate on your Client Access server post deployment and change the Outlook Anywhere namespace. You don't need to change the default self-signed SSL certificate on the mailbox servers.

If you are planning to deploy Exchange 2013/2016 in a co-existence scenario in an existing Exchange 2010 environment, you have to enable and configure Outlook Anywhere on all of your legacy Exchange 2010 CAS servers in your organization and choose NTLM as the IIS Authentication method in addition to basic authentication method, as listed in the Exchange Deployment Assistant `https://technet.microsoft.com/en-us/office/dn756393`. Lastly, point your external hostname for Outlook Anywhere to the latest release of Exchange 2013/2016 CAS Servers.

You can use any of the following commands to retrieve the settings of Outlook Anywhere on server called `Exchange01`:

```
Get-OutlookAnywhere -Server Exchange01
```

```
Get-OutlookAnywhere -Identity "Exchange01\rpc (Default Web Site)"
```

Use `Set-OutlookAnywhere` cmdlet to change any of the settings, for example, the external client authentication method, to NTLM:

```
Set-OutlookAnywhere -Identity:"Exchange01\rpc (Default Web Site)"
-ExternalClientAuthenticationMethod NTLM
```

Managing Client Access Servers

In this section, we will configure the Client Access Servers for some of the protocols that you have learned earlier in the chapter.

The following command will set the internal hostname, client authentication method, require SSL, and authentication methods for Outlook Anywhere:

```
Get-OutlookAnywhere | Set-OutlookAnywhere -InternalHostname
"Exchange01.contoso.com" -InternalClientAuthenticationMethod
Ntlm -InternalClientsRequireSsl $true -IISAuthenticationMethods
Negotiate,NTLM,Basic
```

Similarly, OWA, Exchange `ActiveSync`, Exchange Web services, and OAB can be configured using the following commands:

```
Set-OwaVirtualDirectory -Identity "Exchange01\owa (Default Web Site)"
-ExternalUrl https://mail.contoso.com/ow

Set-ActiveSyncVirtualDirectory -Identity "Exchange01\Microsoft-Server-
ActiveSync (Default Web Site)" -ExternalUrl "https://mail.contoso.com/
Microsoft-Server-ActiveSync"

Set-WebServicesVirtualDirectory -Identity "Exchange01\EWS (Default Web
Site)" -ExternalUrl https://mail.contoso.com/EWS/Exchange.asmx

Set-OABVirtualDirectory -Identity "Exchange01\OAB (Default Web Site)"
-ExternalUrl "https://mail.contoso.com/OAB"
```

The command sets the service connection point for the `Autodiscover` service:

```
Set-ClientAccessServer -Identity Exchange01
-AutoDiscoverServiceInternalURI https://autodiscover.contoso.com/
AutoDiscover/AutoDiscover.xml
```

Managing transport connectors

Transport connectors are used to control the routing of inbound and outbound emails. There are two types of connectors in Exchange: Send and Receive connectors

Send connector

This connector is used for outbound mail flow from Mailbox Servers. They are commonly used to transfer e-mail messages either to a smart host or directly to the recipient e-mail server using DNS.

You can retrieve the settings and configure and create new send connectors using the `Get-SendConnector`, `Set-SendConnector`, and `New-SendConnector` cmdlets.

The following command will display information about the Send connector named Internet:

```
Get-SendConnector "Internet" | Format-List
```

The `FrontendProxyEnabled` parameter of the `Set-SendConnector` cmdlet is used to route outbound e-mails through the CAS server role. The following example sets the `FrontendProxyEnabled` parameter to `$true` on a Send connector, which simplifies the outbound e-mail flow, especially if you are managing a large number of Exchange Servers:

```
Set-SendConnector "Internet" -FrontendProxyEnabled $true
```

The following command creates a new send connector with the address space of `fabrikam.com`. So, messages sent to recipients in the `fabrikam.com` domain will use this new connector:

```
New-SendConnector -Internet -Name Fabrikam -AddressSpaces fabrikam.com
```

Receive connector

This connector is used to control the inbound mail flow of your organization. By default, receive connectors are created on Client Access and the Mailbox server role in Exchange 2013/2016.

Receive connectors listen on a local IP address and port from a range of remote IP addresses. You can configure remote IP ranges and authentication settings if you want to control which servers can send e-mails to your Exchange organization:

We will use `Get-ReceiveConnector`, `Set-ReceiveConnector`, and `New-ReceiveConnector` to retrieve, modify, and create new Receive connector

The example will list all the receive connectors on server `Exchange01`:

```
Get-ReceiveConnector -Server Exchange01
```

The following command will set the banner for the Internet receive connector:

```
Set-ReceiveConnector -Identity "Default Frontend Exchange01" -Banner "220
SMTP OK"
```

If you want to create a new receive connector with a custom IP range, you can use the `New-ReceiveConnector` cmdlet:

```
New-ReceiveConnector -Name Relay -Usage Custom -Bindings
192.168.10.101:25 -RemoteIPRanges 192.168.10.1-192.168.10.5
```

Managing DSN Messages

Delivery Status Notification (DSN) is used to send Non-Delivery Reports (NDRs) to messages senders. There are lots of in-built DSN messages that one can use in Exchange 2013/2016 or create custom DSN messages if the built-in DSN messages do not suit your organizations requirements. The `*-SystemMessage` cmdlets are used to manage DSN in Exchange.

To retrieve a list of all built-in DSN messages, run the following command

```
Get-SystemMessage -Original
```

To view a list of all Custom DSN messages, type the following:

`Get-SystemMessage`

The following command creates a custom plain text DSN message 5.2.2 sent to internal recipients in English:

```
PS C:\> New-SystemMessage -Internal $true -Language En -DSNCode 5.2.2 -Text "You tried to send a
 message to a recipient whose mailbox is full and is no longer accepting messages. Please contac
t Helpdesk at extension 5004 for assistance"

Identity                        Text
--------                        ----
en\Internal\5.2.2               You tried to send a message to a recipient whose mailbox is full a...
```

You can use `Set-SystemMessage` to change the properties of the existing custom DSN:

```
PS C:\> Set-SystemMessage En\Internal\5.2.2 -Text "The mailbox you tried to send an e-mail messa
ge is full. Please contact Help Desk at extension 5004 for assistance"
PS C:\>
```

Finally, use `Remove-SystemMessage` to remove the custom DSN message:

`Remove-SystemMessage En\Internal\5.2.2`

If you want to monitor your custom DSN and want it to be copied to a mailbox, use the following commands to associate an Exchange recipient with the `MicrosoftExchagneRecipientReplyRecipient` parameter:

`Set-OrganizationConfig -MicrosoftExchangeRecipientReplyRecipient "System Mailbox - Contoso"`

Then, use the `Set-TransportConfig` command to add/remove your custom DSN to the monitor:

`Set-TransportConfig -GenerateCopyOfDSNFor @{Add="5.2.2"; Remove="5.5.6"}`

Managing Message tracking logs

In Exchange Server 2013/2016, message tracking is enabled by default and you can use the `Set-TransportService` and `Set-MailboxServer` cmdlets to configure various message tracking configuration tasks. The tracking log files exist in the `%Exchangeinstallpath%TransportRoles\Logs\MessageTracking` folder.

Here are different log files created in this folder:

MSGTRK	Transport service logs
MSGTRKMA	Moderated transport logs for example, approvals and rejections if enabled
MSGTRKMD	Logs messages delivered to mailboxes using the Mailbox Transport Delivery Service
MSGTRKMS	Logs messages sent from mailboxes using the Mailbox Transport Submission service

These logs are stored in the directory using the following naming convention `MSGTRXMDyyyymmdd-nnnn.log` where `yyyymmdd` is the coordinated Universal time when the log file is created, and `nnnn` is the instance number, which starts at 1 every day for each message-tracking log file named prefix. Exchange uses circular logging for better disk capacity management. It deletes log files that are older than a specified number of days or when the maximum size of the message tracking directory is reached. Both these settings can be configured.

You need first understand the following items used in message tracking log files:

- **Fields**: date-time, client-ip, client-hostname, server-ip, server-hostname, Source, Event-id, Original-client-ip, and so on
- **Event Name**: BADMAIL, DEFER, DELIVER, SEND, RECEIVE, DSN, and so on
- **Source**: DNS, Gateway, MailboxRule, PICKUP, ROUTING, SMTP, and so on

 Refer to the Exchange 2013/2016 online documentation available at `https://technet.microsoft.com/en-us/library/bb124375(v=exchg.150).aspx` for details.

The following command will search the message tracking logs and return the first 1000 Receive events. It then formats the objects in the list format and redirects the fields starting with only Send and Recipient to the file called `C:\Tracking\RecipientSearch.txt` file.

There are some differences in the output of the `Get-MessageTrackingLog` cmdlet and the field in the message tracking logs. For example, in the output, you will see that date-time field is displayed as Timestamp; the recipient-address field is displayed as Recipients; and the sender-address field is displayed as Sender. Dashes — (-) are removed from the field names such as internal-message-id will list as `InternalMessageId`:

```
Get-MessageTrackingLog -EventId Send | Format-List Send*,Recipient* /
"C:\Tracking\RecipientSearch.txt"
```

If you know a message ID and want to search it against multiple Exchange Servers in your organization, then the following command will display the desired output for you:

```
Get-ExchangeServer | where {$_.isHubTransportServer -eq $true -or
$_.isMailboxServer -eq $true} | Get-MessageTrackingLog -MessageId
c78b459b-8b65-46cb-9383-e1849e60663e@Exchange01.contoso.com | Select-
Object Timestamp,ServerHostname,ClientHostname,Source,EventId,Recipients
| Sort-Object -Property Timestamp
```

Managing transport queues

A queue is a temporary storage location for messages in Exchange before they proceed to the next step of processing or delivery. In Exchange 2013/2016, the following types of queues are used:

- **Persistent queues**: They exist on every transport server in the organization and are of the following types:
    - **Submission queue**: Categorizer uses this queue to collect all the messages that need to be resolved, processed, and routed by the different transport agents
    - **Unreachable queue**: This queue is for messages that Exchange cannot route to the destination
    - **Poison message queue**: This queue holds messages that the Exchange system thinks is harmful for the environment after a crash of the transport server or service

- **Delivery queues**: These queues and dynamically created and removed when empty and is used to hold messages in transit, which are in the process of being delivered to either local or remote destinations using the SMTP protocol.

- **Shadow queues**: They hold redundant copies of a message in transit to ensure that messages are not lost in transit due to a transport server or service failure.

- **Safety Net**: This holds the copies of messages delivered by the transport server. This is not accessible by the queue viewer and cmdlets.

All the preceding queues are stored in one ESE database in the `%ExchangeInstallP ath%TransportRoles\data\Queue folder`. Like any ESE database, all transactions are written to log files in memory and then later committed to the database. The checkpoint file is used to keep track of transaction logs, which are committed to the database. The queue database uses circular logging to retain storage space and ensure that the transaction logs do not use the entire disk space. This means that older transaction logs, which are committed to the database, are automatically deleted, and they cannot be used to recover a queue database from backup.

You can modify different options for the queue database by editing the file located at `%ExchangeInstallPath%Bin\EdgeTransport.exe.config`. Once you make changes to the file, you have to restart the Microsoft Exchange Transport service. Under the `<appSettings>` section in the file, you can configure settings such as `QueueDatabaseLoggingPath`, `QueueDatabasePath`, `QueueDatabaseOnlineDefragSchedule`, and more.

 For details, refer to the Exchange 2013/2016 online documentation available at `https://technet.microsoft.com/en-us/ library/bb125177(v=exchg.150).aspx`.

You can manage the queue through either the Queue Viewer utility or the `*-queue` cmdlets. These utilities will allow you to manage queues only on a single server.

Examples

The following command will display all the non-empty queues on Mailbox Server named `Exchange01`:

```
Get-Queue -Server Exchange01 -Exclude Empty
```

If you want to find information about queues holding more than 50 messages on the Mailbox Server, type the following:

```
Get-Queue -Filter {MessageCount -gt 50} | Format-List
```

This suspends the queue called `fabrikam.com` on Mailbox Server `Exchange01`:

```
Suspend-Queue -Identity Exchange01\fabrikam.com
```

The following commands will resume/retry a suspended queue called `fabrikam. com` on `Exchange01`:

```
Resume-Queue -Identity Exchange01\fabrikam.com
Retry-Queue -Identity Exchange01\fabrikam.com
```

You can resubmit messages using the following cmdlet with the Resubmit parameter. This resubmits all the messages from any queue with the status of Retry on Exchange01:

```
Retry-Queue -Filter {Status -eq "Retry"} -Server Exchange01 -Resubmit
$true
```

The Get-QueueDigest cmdlet provides a summary view of all the queues on all servers in a specific scope such as an Active Directory site, a Database Availability Group, or a specific Edge server. The default setting for Get-QueueDigest is to display results between one and two minutes. This can be configured by the QueueLoggingInterval key in the EdgeTransport.exe.config and QueueDiagnosticsAggregationInterval parameters on Set-TransportConfig. Both these values are set to 1 minute by default.

The following example will display a summary of all the queues on Exchange Mailbox servers in the Active Directory site named Portland where the message count is greater than 50:

```
Get-QueueDigest -Site Portland -Filter {MessageCount -gt 50}
```

Another example where it will display the summary information of all the queues on Mailbox servers which are part of Database Availability Group DAG01 and the queue status is set to retry:

```
Get-QueueDigest -Dag DAG01 -Filter {Status -eq "Retry"}
```

Managing Public Folder Mailboxes

The Public folder architecture has been overhauled in Exchange 2013, and the new architecture is being used in Exchange 2016 as well. Compared to the previous releases of Exchange, Public folders in Exchange 2013 now use the mailbox infrastructure. This helps in utilizing the existing high availability and disaster recovery techniques used for Public folders. There is no public folder database in Exchange 2013/2016; instead, we have public folder mailboxes that store hierarchy and content.

There are primary and secondary hierarchy mailboxes with the difference that one stores a writable copy of the public folder hierarchy, while the other stores the read-only copy. Both of these mailboxes can also store content in them.

The management of Public folders can be done by the Exchange Admin Center and Exchange management shell. In the Exchange management shell, these are the following parameters added to support Public folders with the `*-Mailbox` cmdlets:

- `PublicFolder`: This parameter is used to create a public folder mailbox using the `New-Mailbox` cmdlet.

  The following command creates a public folder mailbox called `PrimaryHierarchy`:

  `New-Mailbox -PublicFolder -Name PrimaryHierarchy`

  You can create multiple secondary hierarchy mailboxes for load balancing:

  `New-Mailbox -PublicFolder -Name NorthAmericasPF`

  In order to verify that the primary hierarchy mailbox is created, run the following command:

  `Get-OrganizationConfig | Format-List RootPublicFolderMailbox`

- `HoldForMigration`: This is used only if you migrate public folders from exchange 2007 or Exchange 2010. You will use the `*MigrationBatch` and `*PublicFolderMigrationRequest` cmdlets along with a few scripts such as `Export-PublicFolderStatistics.ps1` and `PublicFolderToMailboxMapGenerator.ps1`, which are available with the installation of Exchange in the `%ExchangeInstallPath%Scripts` folder. This is as far as we go for public folder migration as this is beyond the scope of this book.

- `IsHierarchyReady`: This parameter states that a particular mailbox is ready to share hierarchy with users. This is set to `$True` if the hierarchy is synched to this particular mailbox.

- `IsExcludedFromServingHierarchy`: This parameter can be set and is used to exclude a particular public folder mailbox to be used for hierarchy to users.

If `DefaultPublicFolderMailbox` is set on the user mailbox to a particular public folder mailbox, the user will still access a public folder mailbox irrespective of the values set for the parameters called `IsHierarchyReady` and `IsExcludedFromServingHierarchy`.

The Public folder content such as emails, posts, documents, forms, and so on are stored in the public folder mailbox, but this content is not replicated across multiple mailboxes. It means that users who want to access a particular content has to access a specific public folder mailbox that hosts the content. The public folder content is not indexed by the Exchange search.

If you want to move a single public folder or the entire branch of public folders from one mailbox to another, you can use the `*-PublicFolderMoveRequest` cmdlets. The same set of cmdlets will also help you move public folder mailboxes from one Mailbox Database to another. The preceding cmdlet will move the content asynchronously.

The following example will move the public folder called Sales leads from the public folder mailbox Sales to `NASales01`:

```
New-PublicFolderMoveRequest -Folders \Sales\Salesleads -TargetMailbox
NASales01
```

You can use the same cmdlet to multiple folders separated with commas

```
New-PublicFolderMoveRequest -Folders \Sales\WebInquiries,\Sales\
Salesleads,\Sales\GeneralInquiries -TargetMailbox NASales01
```

If you have a large number of public folder branches that need to be relocated to a different mailbox, use the `Move-PublicFolderBranch.ps1` script from the `%ExchangeInstallPath%` Script folder:

```
C:\Program Files\Microsoft\Exchange Server\V15\Scripts/ .\Move-
PublicFolderBranch.ps1 -FolderRoot \Sales -TargetPublicFolderMailbox
NASales01
```

The status of the following cmdlet will tell you whether the move has completed or not:

```
Get-PublicFolderMoveRequest | Format-List Status
```

Writing a basic script

We will write a simple script to report various Mailbox and Client Access settings such as Database Name, `ActiveSyncMailboxPolicy`, `DisplayName`, `EmailAddress`, `LastSuccessSync` time, and more for users with Exchange mailboxes.

The first step is to create a variable called `$Usermailboxes` that will store a list of all the user mailboxes in the organization. Then, we have declared `$Report` as an empty array to store objects for later purposes in the script. We then use another `ForEach` to loop through each of the mailboxes and define a few additional variables to store various Mailbox and CAS settings for the mailboxes. `$MailboxObject` is a new `PSObject` created with our required properties using the `Add-Member` cmdlet. Finally, the report will be exported to a CSV file in the `C:\Scripts` folder with today's `date.csv` format.

You can also add HTML formatting and send an e-mail to the administrators using a scheduled task:

```
$UserMailboxes = Get-Mailbox -ResultSize Unlimited
$Report = @()
foreach ($Mailbox in $UserMailboxes)

{

$CASSettings = Get-CasMailbox -identity $Mailbox
$MBXSettings = Get-Mailbox -Identity $Mailbox
$MBXStats = Get-MailboxStatistics -Identity $Mailbox
$ActiveSyncStats = Get-MobileDeviceStatistics -Mailbox $Mailbox

$MailboxObject = New-Object PSObject

$MailboxObject | Add-Member -MemberType NoteProperty -Name
"DisplayName" -Value $MBXSettings.DisplayName
$MailboxObject | Add-Member -MemberType NoteProperty -Name
"EmailAddress" -Value $MBXSettings.PrimarySmtpAddress
$MailboxObject | Add-Member -MemberType NoteProperty -Name
"ServerName" -Value $MBXStats.ServerName
$MailboxObject | Add-Member -MemberType NoteProperty -Name
"DatabaseName" -Value $MBXStats.DatabaseName
$MailboxObject | Add-Member -MemberType NoteProperty -Name
"MailboxSize" -Value $MBXStats.TotalItemSize
$MailboxObject | Add-Member -MemberType NoteProperty -Name "ItemCount"
-Value $MBXStats.ItemCounts
$MailboxObject | Add-Member -MemberType NoteProperty -Name
"ActiveSyncMailboxPolicy" -Value $CASSettings.ActiveSyncMailboxPolicy
$MailboxObject | Add-Member -MemberType NoteProperty -Name
"DeviceType" -Value $ActiveSyncStats.DeviceType
$MailboxObject | Add-Member -MemberType NoteProperty -Name
"LastSyncAttemptTime" -Value $ActiveSyncStats.LastSyncAttemptTime
$MailboxObject | Add-Member -MemberType NoteProperty -Name
"LastSuccessSync" -Value $ActiveSyncStats.LastSuccessSync

$Report += $MailboxObject

}

$Report = $Report | Select-Object DisplayName, EmailAddress,
ServerName, DatabaseName, MailboxSize, ItemCount,
ActiveSyncMailboxPolicy, DeviceType, LastSyncAttemptTime,
LastSuccessSync | Export-Csv -Encoding default -NoTypeInformation
-Path "C:\Scripts\$(get-date -Format "dd-MM-yyyy").csv"
```

Summary

In this chapter, we covered the configuration of different Exchange server roles and services such as Mailbox, Client Access, and Transport. You learned the usage of Exchange ActiveSync, Outlook Anywhere, and the POP and IMAP protocols to connect to Exchange mailboxes. You also learned to configure the mail flow using transport connectors and creating and managing delivering Status Notifications, Message Tracking logs, and managing Public folders.

In the next chapter, we will review auditing and discovery features in Exchange.

7
Auditing and E-Discovery

In this chapter, we are going to discuss about the new features in Exchange 2013 and 2016 release that will help organizations meet their compliance and E-discovery requirements.

Let's learn about the Auditing and E-discovery features available in Exchange 2013 and online.

The following topics will be covered in this chapter:

- New features in Exchange 2016
- The In-place hold
- Retrieving and exporting e-mails for Auditing
- Retrieving content using KQL queries
- Searching and removing e-mails from the server
- Enabling Auditing and understanding its usage
- Writing a basic script

New features in Exchange 2016

Let's review different features in Exchange 2013 and 2016 that can be used by organizations to meet their compliance requirements:

- **The In-Place hold**: In Exchange 2010, when a mailbox is enabled for a feature called the Litigation hold, all mailbox data will be stored until the hold is removed. With Exchange 2013 and 2016 the In-place hold allows the Administrators granularity compared to the Litigation hold feature in Exchange 2010. Now, administrators can choose what to hold and for how long the hold to work.

- **In Place E-Discovery**: In Exchange 2010, when you run a discovery search, it will copy the items matching the searched criteria into a discovery mailbox from which you can export it to a PST file or provide access to a group of people. In Exchange, when you run the discovery search, you can see the results live from your search. You will also get an option to create a saved search to be used later with minor modifications if required.

- **Audit logs**: In Exchange 2013 and 2016, you can enable two types of audit logging:
  - **Administrator audit logs**: Administrator audit logs will record any action performed by the administrator using tools such as Exchange Admin Center and Exchange management shell
  - **Mailbox Audit logs**: Mailbox audit logs can be enabled for individual mailboxes and will store the log entries in their Recoverable items audits subfolder

The In-Place hold

The Exchange 2013 and 2016 release allows admins to create granular hold policies by allowing them to preserve items in the mailbox using the following scenarios:

- **Indefinite hold**: This feature is called Litigation hold in Exchange 2010, and it allows mailbox items to be stored indefinitely. The items in this case are never deleted. It can be used where a group of users are working on some highly sensitive content that might need a review later.

  The following example sets the mailbox for Amy Alberts on the Litigation hold (in Exchange 2010) for indefinite hold:

  ```
  Set-Mailbox -Identity amya -LitigationHoldEnabled $True
  ```

  In Exchange 2013 and 2016, you will need to use the New-MailboxSearch cmdlet without any parameters as shown next to get the same results:

  ```
  New-MailboxSearch "Amy mailbox hold" -SourceMailboxes "amya@
  contoso.com" -InPlaceHoldEnabled $True
  ```

The same can be achieved using the In-place E-discovery and hold wizard in Exchange Admin Center as shown in the following screenshot:

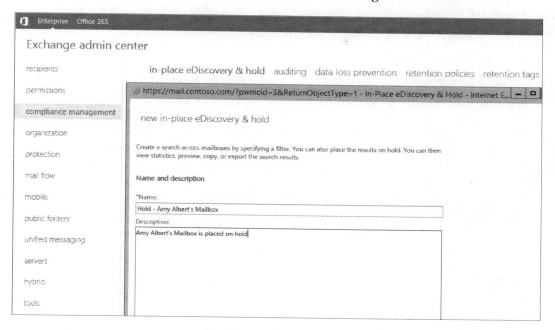

- **The Query-based hold**: Using this, you can specify keywords, dates, message types, and recipient addresses, and only the one's specified in the query will be stored. This is useful if you don't want to enable all your mailboxes for indefinite hold.

- **The Time-based hold**: This will allow admins to hold items during a specific period. The duration is calculated from the date and time the item is received or created.

In order to modify the In-place or Litigation hold properties on mailboxes, you need to be a member of Discovery Management RBAC Role Group that we have covered it in *Chapter 4, Exchange Security*.

The following example creates a Query-based and Time-based In-place hold for all the mailboxes that are part of the distribution group Group-Finance and hold every e-mail, meeting, or IM that contains the keywords Merger and Acquisition for 2 years:

```
New-MailboxSearch "Acquisition-Merger" -SourceMailboxes Group-Finance
-InPlaceHoldEnabled $True -ItemHoldPeriod 730 -SearchQuery '"Merger" and
"Acquisition"' -MessageTypes Ema il,Meetings,IM
```

The Recoverable items folder in each mailbox is used to store items using litigation and In-place hold. The subfolders used to store items are Deletions, Purges, Discovery holds, and versions. The versions folder is used to make a copy of the items before making changes using a process called as copy-on-write. This ensures that the original as well as modified copies of the items are stored in the versions folder. All these items are indexed by Exchange search and returned by the In-Place discovery search.

The Recoverable items folder has its own storage quota, and it's different for Exchange 2013/2016 and Exchange online. For Exchange 2013 and 2016 deployments, the default value of `RecoverableItemsWarningQuota` and `RecoverableItemsQuota` are set to 20 GB and 30 GB respectively. These properties can be managed using the `Set-MailboxDatabase` and `Set-Mailbox` cmdlets. It is critical for administrators to monitor your quota messages logged in the Application event logs as users will not be able to permanently delete items, nor they will be able to empty the deleted items folder if the Recoverable Items Quota is reached. The copy-on-write feature will not work for obvious reasons.

 For Exchange online, if a mailbox is placed on litigation hold, the size of the Recoverable items folder is set to 100 GB.

If email forwarding is enabled for mailboxes, which are on hold and a message is forwarded without a copy to the original mailbox, Exchange 2013 will not capture that message. However, if the mailbox is on Exchange 2016 or Exchange online, and the message that is forwarded meets the hold criteria for the mailbox, a copy of the message will be saved in the Recoverable items folder and can be searched using the E-Discovery search later on.

Retrieving and exporting e-mails for Auditing using In-Place E-discovery

Now, we have seen how to place mailboxes on hold. In this topic, you will learn how to search and retrieve mailbox items using the E-discovery search in Exchange 2013, 2016 and Exchange online. The In-place eDiscovery and hold wizard in Exchange Admin Center allows authorized users to search the content based on sender, recipient, keywords, start, and end dates. The administrators can then take the actions such as estimating, previewing, copying, and exporting search results.

The following screenshot shows an example of a search result:

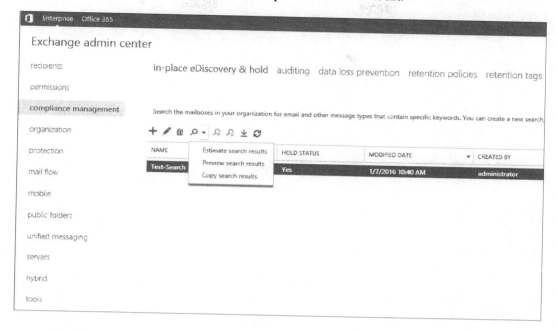

Search starting Exchange 2013 uses Microsoft Search Foundation with better indexing and querying functionalities and performances. As the same search foundation is used with SharePoint and other Office products, the e-discovery search can now be performed from both Exchange and SharePoint environments with the same results. The query language used by In-Place eDiscovery is **Keyword Query Language (KQL)**, which you will learn in the next section.

The following screenshot shows how to use the search query using KQL syntax and time range fields:

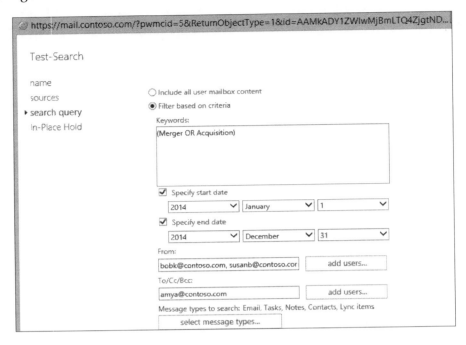

You can also specify the message types to be returned in the search results as shown in the following screenshot:

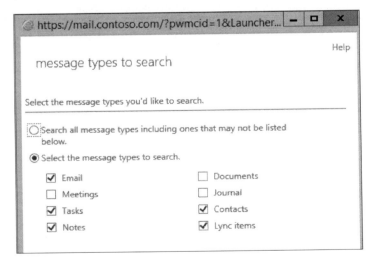

Once you have estimated the search items, you can then preview and export the items to a PST file or a discovery mailbox as shown in the following screenshot:

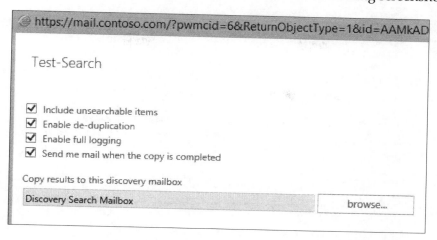

Now, as this book is about managing Exchange using PowerShell, let's see how to use the same query in PowerShell using `New-MailboxSearch` cmdlet. Here, `-SourceMailboxes` will define mailboxes to be searched between 1st January 2014 to 31st December 2014 using the `-StartDate` and `-EndDate` parameters. The `-SearchQuery` parameter is used for **KQL (Keyword Query Language)** with words such as Merger or Acquisition. The results will be copied to the Legal-Mergers discovery mailbox specified using the `-TargetMailbox` parameter. Finally, status reports are sent to the group called `legal@contoso.com` when the search is completed and specified using the `-StatusMailRecipient` parameter:

```
New-MailboxSearch "Acquisition-Merger" -SourceMailboxes bobk@contoso.
com,susanb@contoso.com -SearchQuery '"Merger" OR "Acquisition"'
-TargetMailbox Legal-Mergers -StartDate "01/01/2014" -EndDate
"12/31/2014" -StatusMailRecipients legal@contoso.com
```

Retrieving content using KQL queries

KQL consists of free text keywords including words, phrases, and property restrictions. KQL queries are case-insensitive, but the operators are not and have to be specified in uppercase. A free text expression in a KQL query can be a word without any spaces or punctuation or a phrase enclosed in double quotation marks.

The following examples will return the content that have the words **Merger** and **Acquisition**:

```
merger acquisition
merge* acquisition
acquistion merg*
```

It is important to note that KQL queries do not support suffix matching. This means you cannot use a wildcard (*) operator before a word or phrase in a KQL query.

We can use Property restrictions in a KQL query in the following format. There should not be any space between the Property name, the Property operator, and the Property value:

`<Property Name><Property Operator><Property Value>`

For example, author "John Doe" will return content whose author is John Doe;

`filetype:xlsx` will return Excel spreadsheets; and title:"KQL Query" will return results with the content KQL query in the title:

You can combine these property restrictions to build complex KQL queries.

For example, the following query will return the content authored by John Doe or Jane Doe. It can be used in the following formats. Both the formats will return the same results:

`author:"John Doe" author:"Jane Doe"`

`author:"John Doe" OR author:"Jane Doe"`

If you want to search for all the word documents authored by Jane Doe, you will use either of the formats:

`author:"Jane Doe" filetype:docx`

`author:"Jane Doe" AND filetype:docx`

Now let's take a look at the use of the Proximity operators called NEAR and ONEAR, which are used to search items in close proximity to each other.

The NEAR operator matches the results where the search terms are in close proximity without preserving the order of the terms:

`<expression> NEAR(n=5) <expression>`

Here, n >= 0 with a default value of 8 indicates the maximum distance used between the terms; for example, merger NEAR acquistion.

This will return results where the word `merger` is followed by `acquisition` and vice versa by up to eight other words.

If you want to find content where the term `acquisition` is followed by the term `merger` for up to five terms but not the other way round, use the ONEAR operator that maintains the order of the terms specified in the query. The syntax is the same as the NEAR operator with a default value of `n = 8`:

```
"acquisition" ONEAR(n=5) "merger"
```

Searching and removing e-mails from the server

There will be times when you as an Exchange administrator would get request to log or delete specific items from the user's mailboxes. The `Search-Mailbox` cmdlet helps you to search a mailbox or a group of mailboxes for a specific item, and it also allows you to delete them.

You need to be part of the Mailbox Search and Mailbox Import Export RBAC roles to be able to search and delete messages from a user's mailbox.

The following example searches John Doe's mailbox for e-mails with the subject "Credit Card Statement" and logs the result in the Mailbox Search Log folder in the administrator's mailbox:

```
Search-Mailbox -Identity "John Doe" -SearchQuery 'Subject:"Credit Card
statement"' -TargetMailbox administrator -TargetFolder "MailboxSearchLog"
-LogOnly -LogLevel Full
```

The following example searches all mailboxes for attachments that have "Virus" as the file name and logs it in the Mail box Search log in the administrator's mailbox:

```
Get-Mailbox -ResultSize unlimited | Search-Mailbox -SearchQuery
attachment:virus* -TargetMailbox administrator -TargetFolder
"MailboxSearchLog" -LogOnly -LogLevel Full
```

You can use the search mailbox to delete content as well. For example, the following cmdlet will delete all e-mails with subject line "Test Email" from Amy Albert's mailbox:

```
Search-Mailbox -Identity "Amy Albert" -SearchQuery 'Subject:"Test Email"'
-DeleteContent
```

If you want to keep a back up of Amy Albert's mailbox content to a "BackupMailbox" before permanently deleting it, use the following command:

```
Search-Mailbox -Identity "Amy Albert" -SearchQuery 'Subject:"Test Email"'
-TargetMailbox "BackupMailbox" -TargetFolder "amya-DeletedMessages"
-LogLevel Full -DeleteContent
```

Enable Auditing and understanding its usage

We will discuss the following two types of audit logs available in Exchange 2013:

- Administrator audit logs
- Mailbox audit logs

Administrator audit logs

Administrator audit logs are used to log when a cmdlet is executed from Exchange Management Shell or Exchange Admin Center except the cmdlets that are used to display information such as the Get-* and Search-* cmdlets. By default, Administrator audit log is enabled for new Exchange 2013/2016 installations. The admin audit log is a built-in cmdlet extension agent that we have covered in *Chapter 2, Learning Recipient Management* This agent reads the audit log configuration and evaluates each cmdlet when they are run, and then it logs it based on the configuration.

The following command will audit all cmdlets. Note that this is the default behavior. So, if this is a new installation of Exchange 2013 and 2016, you don't have to make any changes. You have to only run this if you have made some changes using the Set-AdminAuditLogConfig cmdlet earlier:

```
Set-AdminAuditLogConfig -AdminAuditLogCmdlets *
```

Now, let's say you have a group of delegated administrators managing your Exchange environment, and you want to ensure that all the management tasks are logged. For example, you want to audit cmdlets that make changes to the mailbox, distribution groups, and management roles. You will type the following cmdlet:

```
Set-AdminAuditLogConfig -AdminAuditLogCmdlets *Mailbox,*Management*,*Dist
ributionGroup*
```

The previous command will audit the cmdlets along with the specified parameters. You can take this a step further by specifying which parameters you want to monitor. For example, you are trying to understand why there is an unequal distribution of mailboxes in your databases and incorrect entries in the Custom Attribute properties for your user mailboxes. You will run the following command that will only monitor these two properties:

```
Set-AdminAuditLogConfig -AdminAuditLogParameters Database,Custom*
```

By default, 90 days is the age of the audit logs and can be changed using the `-AdminAuditLogAgeLimit` parameter. The following command sets the audit login age to 2 years:

```
Set-AdminAuditLogConfig -AdminAuditLogAgeLimit 730.00:00:00
```

By default, the cmdlet with a Test verb is not logged as it generates lot of data. But, if you are troubleshooting an issue and want to keep a record of it for a later review, you can enable them using this:

```
Set-AdminAuditLogConfig -TestCmdletLoggingEnabled $True
```

Disabling and enabling to view the admin audit log settings can be done using the following commands:

```
Set-AdminAuditLogConfig -AdminAuditLogEnabled $False
```

```
Set-AdminAuditLogConfig -AdminAuditLogEnabled $True
```

```
Get-AdminAuditLogConfig
```

Once Auditing is enabled, you can search the audit logs using the Search-`AdminAuditLog` and `New-AdminAuditLogsearch cmdlets`. The following example will search the logs for the `Set-Mailbox` cmdlets with the following parameters from 1st January 2014 to 1st December 2014 for users—Holly Holt, Susan Burk, and John Doe:

```
Search-AdminAuditLog -Cmdlets Set-Mailbox -Parameters ProhibitSendQuota,P
rohibitSendReceiveQuota,IssueWarningQuota -StartDate 01/01/2014 -EndDate
12/01/2014 -UserIds hollyh,susanb,johnd
```

This command will search for any changes made to Amy Albert's mailbox configuration from 1st July to 1st October 2015:

```
Search-AdminAuditLog -StartDate 07/01/2015 -EndDate 10/01/2015 -ObjectID
contoso.com/Users/amya
```

This cmdlet is similar to the previous cmdlet with one difference that it uses the parameter called `-StatusMailRecipients` to send e-mail with the subject line called "Mailbox Properties Changes" to amya@contoso.com:

```
New-AdminAuditLogSearch -Cmdlets Set-Mailbox -Parameters
ProhibitSendQuota, ProhibitSendReceiveQuota, IssueWarningQuota,
MaxSendSize, MaxReceiveSize -StartDate 08/01/2015 -EndDate 10/01/2015
-UserIds hollyh,susanb,johnd -StatusMailRecipients amya@contoso.com -Name
"Mailbox Properties changes"
```

Mailbox audit logs

Mailbox audit logging feature in Exchange 2013 and 2016 allows you to log mailbox access by owners, delegates, and administrators. They are stored in Recoverable Items in the Audits subfolder. By default, the logs are retained for up to 90 days. You need to use `Set-Mailbox` with the `AuditLogAgeLimit` parameter to increase the retention period of the audit logs.

The following command will enable mailbox audit logging for John Doe's mailbox, and the logs will be retained for 6 months:

```
Set-Mailbox -Identity "John Doe" -AuditEnabled $true -AuditLogAgeLimit
180.00:00:00
```

The command disables audit logging for Holly Holt's mailbox:

```
Set-Mailbox -Identity "Holly Holt" -AuditEnabled $false
```

If you just want to log the `SendAs` and `SendOnBehalf` actions on Susan Burk's mailbox, type this:

```
Set-Mailbox -Identity "Susan Burk" -AuditDelegate SendAs,SendOnBehalf
-AuditEnabled $true
```

The following command logs the Hard Delete action by the Mailbox owner for Amy Albert's mailbox:

```
Set-Mailbox -Identity "Amy Albert" -AuditOwner HardDelete -AuditEnabled
$true
```

Now that we have enabled auditing, let's see how to search audit logs for the mailboxes using the `Search-MailboxAuditLog` cmdlet. The following example searches the audit logs for mailboxes of John Doe, Amy Albert, and Holly Holt for the actions performed by logon types called Admin and Delegate from 1st September to 1st October 2015. A maximum of 2,000 results will be displayed as specified by the Result size parameter:

```
Search-MailboxAuditLog -Mailboxes johnd,amya,hollyh -LogonTypes
Admin,Delegate -StartDate 9/1/2015 -EndDate 10/1/2015 -ResultSize 2000
```

You can use pipelines and search the operation of Hard Delete in this example with the Where-Object cmdlet in Susan Burk's mailbox from 1st September to 17th September 2015:

```
Search-MailboxAuditLog -Identity susanb -LogonTypes Owner -ShowDetails
-StartDate 9/1/2015 -EndDate 9/17/2015 | Where-Object {$_.Operation -eq
"HardDelete"}
```

Once you have enabled the mailbox audit logging, you can also use Exchange Admin Center by navigating to **compliance management**, **auditing** tab, and **Run a non-owner mailbox access report...**.

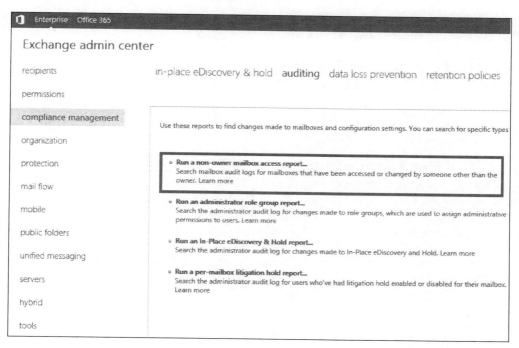

The following screenshot shows the search criteria that you can use to search the mailboxes accessed by non-owners:

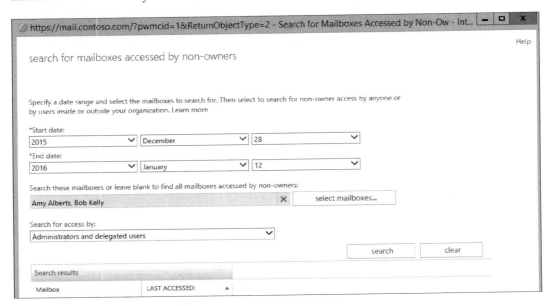

Writing a basic script

As we have seen in the In-Place hold section, the Recoverable Items folder has its own storage quota and has Deletions, Versions, Purges, Audits, Discovery Holds, and Calendar Logging as subfolders. This script will loop through the mailboxes and export the size of these subfolders to a CSV file.

The $Output is an empty array used later to store the output of the script. The $Mbx array stores the list of mailboxes. We then use Foreach to loop through the mailboxes in $Mbx. Note the usage of two if-else statements for the Audits and Discovery Holds section in the script, which are present to ensure that we don't get errors if the user is not enabled for Mailbox Auditing and In-Place holds respectively.

We have created a new object to create a new instance of a PowerShell object and used the Add-Member cmdlet custom Properties to that object and store it in the $report variable for each mailbox in the list. The results are then added to the $Output array defined earlier. Finally, Export-CSV is used to export the output to the Recoverable Items subfolder called size.csv in the current working directory:

```
$Output = @()

Write-Host "Retrieving the List of mailboxes"
$mbx = @(Get-Mailbox -Resultsize Unlimited)

foreach ($Mailbox in $mbx)
{
    $Name = $Mailbox.Name

    Write-Host "Checking $Name Mailbox"

    $AuditsFoldersize = ($mailbox | Get-MailboxFolderStatistics
-FolderScope RecoverableItems | Where {$_.Name -eq "Audits"}).
FolderSize
    if ($AuditsFolderSize -ne $Null) {$AuditsFoldersize} else
{$AuditsFoldersize = 0}

    $DiscoveryHoldsFoldersize = ($mailbox | Get-
MailboxFolderStatistics -FolderScope RecoverableItems | Where {$_.Name
-eq "DiscoveryHolds"}).FolderSize
    if ($DiscoveryHoldsFoldersize -ne $Null)
{$DiscoveryHoldsFoldersize} else {$DiscoveryHoldsFoldersize = 0}

    $PurgesFoldersize = ($mailbox | Get-MailboxFolderStatistics
-FolderScope RecoverableItems | Where {$_.Name -eq "Purges"}).
FolderSize

    $VersionsFoldersize = ($mailbox | Get-MailboxFolderStatistics
-FolderScope RecoverableItems | Where {$_.Name -eq "Versions"}).
FolderSize

    $report = New-Object PSObject
    $report | Add-Member NoteProperty -Name "Name" -Value $Name
    $report | Add-Member NoteProperty -Name "Audits Sub Folder Size"
-Value $AuditsFoldersize
    $report | Add-Member NoteProperty -Name "Deletions Sub Folder
Size" -Value $DeletionsFoldersize
```

```
    $report | Add-Member NoteProperty -Name "DiscoveryHolds Sub Folder
Size" -Value $DiscoveryHoldsFoldersize
    $report | Add-Member NoteProperty -Name "Purges Sub Folder Size"
-Value $PurgesFoldersize
    $report | Add-Member NoteProperty -Name "Versions Sub Folder Size"
-Value $VersionsFoldersize

    $Output += $report

    Write-Host "$Name, $AuditsFoldersize, $DeletionsFoldersize,
$DiscoveryHoldsFoldersize, $PurgesFoldersize, $VersionsFoldersize"
}

Write-Host "Writing output to RecoverableItemssubfolderssize.csv"

$Output | Export-CSV RecoverableItemssubfolderssize.csv
-NoTypeInformation
```

Summary

In this chapter, you learned the use of various types of In-place holds and eDiscovery search. You also learned how they can help organizations meet their regulatory compliance requirements. You learned how to log admin actions and mailbox access by the Administrator audit and the mailbox logging functionality in the Exchange Server 2013/2016 and Exchange online. The tools and cmdlets explained in this chapter will help organizations retain content that is important for them and search and send it to appropriate parties at a later date for a review.

In the next chapter, we will use our knowledge of PowerShell to manage high availability for Exchange 2013 and 2016 Organization.

8

Managing High Availability

The concept of **Database Availability Group (DAG)** was introduced in Exchange 2010, and it has gone through some key improvements in Exchange 2013 and some architectural changes in Exchange 2016. DAG provides the infrastructure to protect the content of your mailbox databases by making copies on other Mailbox servers in your organization, and hence, providing high availability and site resilience.

There is a difference between High Availability and Site Resilience, which is important to understand. We say a messaging system is highly available if all the components are working in a way that if one component fails, the service and the data fails over to one of the working servers automatically. Typically, high availability events are triggered by servers or components failing within a single datacenter. Whereas, in the case of Site Resilience, the service and data is restored with manual intervention from administrators.

In this chapter, you will learn about High Availability and Disaster recovery features available in Exchange Server 2013 and 2016.

The following topics will be covered in this chapter:

- Managing Database Availability Groups
- Managing Database Copies
- Controlling High Availability failover mechanisms
- Database Availability Group health checks
- Database Availability Group Maintenance tasks
- Writing a basic script

Managing Database Availability Groups

Administrators managing and monitoring a highly available deployment of Exchange Servers need to understand some of the key concepts of DAG. In this section, you are going to learn about DAG, Quorum model, and how to add/remove and modify the members of DAG.

A DAG is a collection of up to 16 mailbox servers built at the top of Windows Failover Cluster. We need to understand the concept of quorum before we create our first DAG.

DAG Quorum model

Cluster quorum has been in use for quite some time now in Windows Failover Cluster and the previous releases of Exchange. It is used to ensure that all or majority of the cluster members have a shared and consistent view of the cluster configuration.

When DAG has an even number of nodes, the quorum that is used is the Node and file share majority. It means an external witness server is used as a tie breaker. Let's take an example of four Exchange 2013/2016 Mailbox servers in DAG where every server gets a vote along with the witness server named Exch01, Exch02, Exch03, and Exch04. The fifth server, Server05, is used as a witness server. Now, if Exch01 and Exch03 go down, the cluster still has a majority as Exch03, Exch04, and Server05 are up and running. With Exch01 and Exch02 being down, and if we lose another server Exch04, the quorum will lose its majority and all the databases will be dismounted causing an outage. Then, manual intervention is required to get the required nodes up for majority votes to be established. In this case, it is three votes out of five including the witness server.

With the odd number of nodes in DAG, the quorum model used is node majority where each node gets a vote. So, if one or more node is down, the remaining nodes will check if they can reach the majority of the nodes to keep the cluster up. If they cannot, the services will shut down until an administrator fixes the problem.

DAG can be extended across Active Directory Sites to provide site resilience for your messaging infrastructure. If you are planning to extend DAG members across datacenters, you need to review the impact of the Wide Area Network (WAN) unavailability on the DAG quorum model.

The witness server cannot be a member or DAG and must be in the same Active Directory forest where your DAG is configured. Also, it's worth mentioning that a single witness server can work as a witness for multiple DAGs. In this case, each DAG will have its separate witness directory on the witness server. Also, the Windows firewall exception for file and printer sharing must be set on the witness server.

Creating DAG and adding/removing members

DAG can be created using the Exchange Admin center by navigating to New Database Availability Group wizard or using PowerShell. We will use PowerShell to create a new DAG and add members to it using the `New-DatabaseAvailabilityGroup` and `Add-DatabaseAvailabilityGroupServer` cmdlets. When we use the New-DatabaseAvailabilityGroup cmdlet to create a DAG, a new empty object is created in Active Directory that stores the configuration information about this DAG. We need to specify a unique name, one or multiple IP addresses, or use DHCP to get an IP address for the DAG. We need multiple IP addresses for a DAG that has members spanning across multiple network subnets. The name that you assign to the DAG becomes the cluster administrative access point, which allows name resolution using the cluster IP address.

Starting with DAG members running Exchange 2013 SP1 on Windows Server 2012 R2, you can create a failover cluster without an administrative access point. This means that the cluster will have no IP address and network name resolvable by DNS and no object will be created in Active Directory. It also means that the cluster cannot be managed using the failover cluster manager, and PowerShell cmdlets are used against individual nodes to manage the cluster. You might think of this as a way to reduce the complexity of your DAG management.

It is not supported to convert a DAG, which is configured to use administrative access point, into one which doesn't.

A **cluster name object (CNO)** is created in Active Directory for clusters with administrative access point and is associated with the cluster's name resource. CNO is a Kerberos-enabled object acting as a particular cluster's identity, and it provides its security context. The formation of the Windows Failover cluster and the creation of CNO happened when the first member was added to the DAG. If you are running Windows Server 2012 and later versions, you have to prestage CNO before you add your first member to the DAG. If you are using Windows 2012 R2 servers and want to create a DAG without the cluster administrative access point, you can skip the step of prestating the CNO.

The following example creates a 4-node DAG with a cluster administrative access point. Two servers (Exch1 and Exch2) are on subnet (`192.168.1.0/24`), and the other two servers (Exch3 and Exch4) are on subnet (`192.168.2.0/24`) with Exch5 being the witness server:

```
New-DatabaseAvailabilityGroup -Name DAG01 -WitnessServer Exch5
-DatabaseAvailabilityGroupIPAddresses 192.168.1.10,192.168.2.10

Add-DatabaseAvailabilityGroupServer -Identity DAG01 -MailboxServer Exch1

Add-DatabaseAvailabilityGroupServer -Identity DAG01 -MailboxServer Exch2
```

```
Add-DatabaseAvailabilityGroupServer -Identity DAG01 -MailboxServer Exch3
Add-DatabaseAvailabilityGroupServer -Identity DAG01 -MailboxServer Exch4
```

If you are using Exchange Admin Center to create a DAG without a cluster administrative access point, you have to specify the IP of the DAG as `255.255.255.255` as this is a required parameter, as shown in the screenshot here:

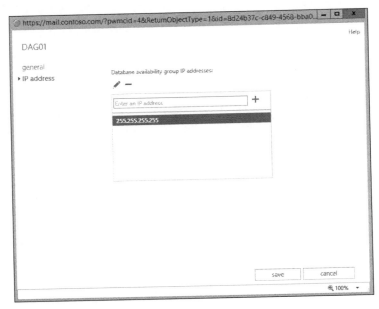

If you are using Exchange Management Shell to create the same DAG without cluster administrative access point, you will use the cmdlets here:

```
New-DatabaseAvailabilityGroup -Name DAG01 -WitnessServer Exch5
-DatabaseAvailabilityGroupIPAddresses ([System.Net.IPAddress])::None
Add-DatabaseAvailabilityGroupServer -Identity DAG01 -MailboxServer Exch1
Add-DatabaseAvailabilityGroupServer -Identity DAG01 -MailboxServer Exch2
Add-DatabaseAvailabilityGroupServer -Identity DAG01 -MailboxServer Exch3
Add-DatabaseAvailabilityGroupServer -Identity DAG01 -MailboxServer Exch4
```

`Remove-DatabaseAvailabilityGroupServer` is used to remove members from a DAG, Mailbox Server `Exch2` is removed from `DAG01` in this case.

```
Remove-DatabaseAvailabilityGroupServer -Identity DAG01 -MailboxServer
Exch2
```

DAG networks

A DAG network is used for two types of traffic—replication and MAPI traffic. We can have a maximum of one **Messaging Application Program Interface (MAPI)** network and one or more replication networks in a DAG. If you have only one network adapter on all of your mailbox servers, which are part of a DAG, the same network will be used for MAPI and replication traffic. You can add multiple network adapters in your DAG members and use one dedicated network for MAPI and others for replication.

DAG networks in Exchange 2013/2016 are automatically configured. If you still need to configure it manually, you need to use the following command for DAG01:

```
Set-DatabaseAvailabilityGroup DAG01 -ManualDagNetworkConfiguration $true
```

If you want to create a new DAG network use the command below:

```
New-DatabaseAvailabilityGroupNetwork -DatabaseAvailabilityGroup DAG01
-Name ReplicationNet2 -Description "Backup Replication Network" -Subnets
192.168.10.0/24 -ReplicationEnabled:$True
```

Adding/removing Database copies

The next step is to create passive copies of the existing mailbox databases using the `Add-MailboxDatabaseCopy` cmdlet:

The following command creates a copy of the MDB1 database on the mailbox server called Exch3:

```
Add-MailboxDatabaseCopy -Identity MDB1 -MailboxServer Exch3
```

Activation Preference is a number between 1 and the number of database copies in a DAG with 1 being the highest priority. This preference number is used by DAG when we redistribute active mailbox databases in a DAG. For example, if you have a DAG with 5 copies of each database, each passive copy can be set with the activation preference numbers of 2, 3, and 4 in this case. This will be used by the DAG Best Copy Selection process if the active copy goes down and there is a tie between two or more passive copies with the same copy queue length.

The following command adds a database copy of MDB2 on the mailbox server called Exch1 with an Activation Preference of 2; and the seeding is postponed for this copy:

```
Add-MailboxDatabaseCopy -Identity MDB2 -MailboxServer Exch1
-ActivationPreference 2 -SeedingPostponed
```

```
Remove-MailboxDatabaseCopy cmdlet is used to remove a database copy MDB1
from server Exch1 in the example below
```

```
Remove-MailboxDatabaseCopy -Identity MDB1\Exch1 -Confirm:$False
```

Managing Database Copies

Once you have created the required number of copies of your databases, you can use Exchange Admin Center or PowerShell to get the status and health of each copy and do other management tasks on them. This is required if you are doing server maintenance or recovering from Exchange server failures.

Suspending/resuming Database copies

If you are planning to run some maintenance tasks on a database copy, you need to suspend the copy first and resume it once the maintenance is complete.

Here are the examples to suspend and resume a database copy:

```
Suspend-MailboxDatabaseCopy -Identity MDB1\Exch3 -SuspendComment
"Replacing Failed Harddrive on Exch3" -Confirm:$False
```

You can suspend the activation of a particular copy as follows:

```
Suspend-MailboxDatabaseCopy -Identity MDB2\Exch1 -ActivationOnly
-Confirm:$False
```

The cmdlet resumes the database copy:

```
Resume-MailboxDatabaseCopy -Identity MDB1\Exch3
```

If you want to resume a database copy without affecting the Activation settings, use the -ReplicationOnly parameter:

```
Resume-MailboxDatabaseCopy -Identity MDB2\Exch1 —ReplicationOnly
```

You can get the activation settings of a particular database called MDB3 using the Get-MailboxDatabaseCopyStatus cmdlet as listed here:

```
Get-MailboxDatabaseCopyStatus MDB3 | Format-List ActivationSuspended
```

If you want to check and set the activation settings of a DAG member called Exch1, use the following commands:

```
Get-MailboxServer Exch1 | Format-List DatabaseCopyAutoActivationPolicy

Set-MailboxServer -Identity Exch1 -DatabaseCopyAutoActivationPolicy
Blocked
```

Database Seeding

There will be times when you need to seed a database from the source. Seeding is a term used to update a database copy from another source. As we have seen earlier, while adding a database copy using the `Add-MailboxDatabaseCopy` cmdlet, we can use the `-SeedingPostponed` parameter to prevent the automatic seeding of the exchange database from the active copy. `Update-MailboxDatabaseCopy` is used to configure the seeding options such as seeding from a specific source. This comes in handy if you have a DAG replicating across a WAN connectivity, and you want to add a new database copy and use a local server for updating the database.

The following example seeds a copy of database `MDB1` on `Exch3` using `Exch2` as the source server:

```
Update-MailboxDatabaseCopy -Identity MDB1\Exch3 -SourceServer Exch2
```

If you have repaired a failed mailbox server called `Exch1` and want to reseed all the databases, type the following:

```
Update-MailboxDatabaseCopy -Server Exch1
```

You can use the Network parameter to specify a network used for seeding. DAG networks are configured to use encryption and compression for communication on different subnets. So, if you want to seed a database from a server that is on a different subnet, you can use the `NetworkCompressionOverride` and `NetworkEncryptionOverride` parameters of the `Update-MailboxDatabaseCopy` cmdlet.

Retrieving and setting Database configuration

Once you have added the database copies, you can view and modify the configuration settings using the `Get-MailboxDatabase`, `Set-MailboxDatabaseCopy`, and `Get-MailboxDatabaseCopyStatus` cmdlets. Before we look at some of the examples, let's review some of the Database settings such as `Replay` and Truncation lag time.

Replay lag time is the amount of time that the Exchange Information store service will wait before replaying log files that are copied to the passive database copy using the replication service. This is used to create lagged copies, which are used to protect against Database and store logical corruptions. The value of the `Replaylagtime` parameter can be set to anywhere between 0-14 days. The default value is 0, which means if you don't specify this parameter, the database copies are not lagged.

Truncation lag time is another setting of a mailbox database copy that defines the time to delay the log deletion for the database copy after the log file has been replayed into the database copy. The time starts when a log file has been copied, inspected, and played into the passive database copy. Log files in Exchange are not truncated from an active copy if you have one or more passive database copies to it, which are in a suspended state. This essentially means that the log files may take a considerable amount of disk space if you don't resume the replication for the passive copies for long periods.

Here are some of the examples of setting the database copy settings.

The following example sets the copy of database MDB2 on Exch1 with a replay and truncation lag time of 1 day and the activation preference of 3 days:

```
Set-MailboxDatabaseCopy -Identity MDB2\Exch1 -ReplayLagTime 1.0:0:0
-TruncationLagTime 1.0:0:0 -ActivationPreference 3
```

If you want to retrieve the information of a database on a particular server, type the following cmdlets:

```
Get-MailboxDatabase -Identity MDB1 -Server Exch2 -Status | Format-List
Get-MailboxDatabaseCopyStatus MDB2 | Format-List
```

Controlling high availability failover mechanisms

While we do database switchovers or they failover automatically, there will be times where the distribution of active database copies across your DAG members will be uneven. For example, you might have a 4 node DAG where 1 member is hosting 10 active copies and other member is hosting only one. This might have an impact on the performance based on server resources. Exchange 2010 and later releases provide the script called RedistributeActiveDatabases.ps1 that will help administrators redistribute the active copies among the DAG members.

The following script will redistribute active database in a DAG based on the activation preference regardless of the copies being hosted on DAG members in another Active Directory site. It will also display a summary once it is complete. The script is located in the %ExchangeInstallPath% Scripts folder:

```
RedistributeActiveDatabases.ps1 -DagName DAG01
-BalanceDbsByActivationPreference -ShowFinalDatabaseDistribution
```

If you just want to activate one of the passive copies to an active copy, use the `Move-ActiveMailboxDatabase` cmdlet. The `MountDialOverride` parameter is used to override the `AutoDatabaseMountDial` setting on the target server and can have the following values:

- **None**: If you use this value the configuration of `AutoDatabaseMountDial` setting will be used on the target server.

- **Lossless**: If you use this value, the database will not mount until all the log files generated on the original active copy have been copied over to the passive copy of the database. This is the default value.

- **GoodAvailability**: This setting will mount the database if up to six log files are missing in the passive copy. This can result in a small amount of data loss.

- **BestAvailability**: This setting will mount the database if up to 12 log files are missing in the passive copy. This can result in data loss.

- **BestEffort**: This setting will mount the database regardless of the number of log files, which are yet to be copied from the original active copy. This can result in a significant amount of data loss.

The following example moves the active database copy of database `MDB1` to `Exch3` with the `MountDialOverride` setting set to `GoodAvailability`:

```
Move-ActiveMailboxDatabase MDB1 -ActivateOnServer Exch3 -MountDialOverrid
e:GoodAvailability
```

At a server level, you can set the value of the `AutoDatabaseMountDial` setting using the `Set-MailboxServer` cmdlet:

```
Set-MailboxServer -Identity Exch2 -AutoDatabaseMountDial GoodAvailability
```

Database Availability Group health checks

In this section, we will review some cmdlets and scripts that are used to collect data, display, and monitor the status of the database copies on DAG members.

The `Get-MailboxDatabaseCopyStatus` cmdlet is used to retrieve the status of the database copies of a particular database and the details of replication networks.

The following example returns the status of all the copies of database `MDB1`:

```
Get-MailboxDatabaseCopyStatus -Identity MDB1 | Format-List
```

The following command will retrieve the status of all databases on Mailbox Server
`Exch2`:

```
Get-MailboxDatabaseCopyStatus -Server Exch2 | Format-List
```

`Test-Replicationhealth` cmdlet displays the replication status of mailbox
database copies. The following example tests the health of replication for the
Mailbox server `Exch3`:

```
Test-ReplicationHealth -Identity Exch3
```

Apart from the preceding cmdlets, you also need to review the events in Event
Viewer and look for crimson channels in the Applications and Services log area.
In the left navigation pane, expand Applications and Services `Log > Microsoft
> Exchange` and review a crimson channel, such as `HighAvailability` or
`MailboxDatabaseFailureItems`, to check the DAG and database copy-related
events as displayed in the image here:

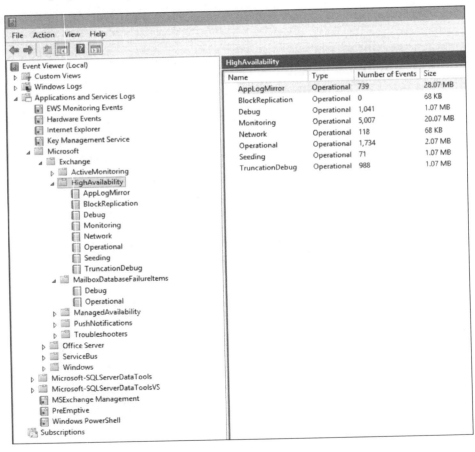

There are scripts available in the %ExchangeInstallPath%Scripts folder that will help you collect information from DAG members event logs. Here are the two scripts that you can use to collect information if you are troubleshooting a DAG-related issue.

- **CollectOverMetrics.ps1**: This script collects information about database, the time stamps of operations, server name, reason, and result of operations and saves it into a CSV file. The script also supports the usage of parameters to change the output and behavior of the script execution.

The example of the following script will collect the information for all the databases matching MOB* in DAG01 and shows the report in an HTML format:

```
CollectOverMetrics.ps1 -DatabaseAvailabilityGroup DAG01 -Database:"MDB*"
-GenerateHTMLReport -ShowHTMLReport
```

If you want to get a summary of events related to databases MDB1 and MDB4, use the following command:

```
CollectOverMetrics.ps1 -SummariseCsvFiles (dir *.csv) -Database MDB1,MDB4
```

- **CollectReplicationMetrics.ps1**: This script is used to collect the data in real time from multiple mailbox servers counters and writes them to a .csv file.

You can use this script to then generate a report in file named as CounterD ata.<ServerName>.<TimeStamp>.csv. The summary report will be saved in the file name as HaReplPerfReport.<DAGName>.<TimeStamp>.csv or HaReplPerfReport.<TimeStamp>.csv if you have not specified the DagName parameter. It uses PowerShell jobs to collect data from servers. It also supports multiple parameters which will change the output and behavior of the script.

The following example will collect 4 hours worth of data from all the members of DAG01 sampled at 1-minute interval, and it will generate a summary report that will be placed in the current working directory:

```
CollectReplicationMetrics.ps1 -DagName DAG01 -Duration "04:00:00"
-Frequency "00:01:00" -ReportPath
```

Database Availability Group Maintenance tasks

In Exchange 2010, we used to use scripts, such as StartDagServerMaintenance. ps1 and StopDagServerMaintenance.ps1, to put a server and get it out of the maintenance mode. In essence, these scripts are used to move all the active databases to another DAG member and mark this server as unavailable.

In Exchange 2013 and 2016, putting a server in maintenance mode will even tell other components, such as Transport or Unified Messaging Call Router, and more, not to send request to that particular server while performing maintenance. This includes moving all the active databases from that server and ensuring that the database doesn't failback during the maintenance. Also, if that server is working as a Primary Active Manager, you need to move the role off the server as well.

Let's understand the role of Active manager before we go any further. On Exchange servers that are members of a DAG, there are two Active Manager Roles **Primary Active Manager (PAM)** and **Standby Active Manager (SAM)**. The role of PAM is to decide which copies will be active and passive copies and get the topology change notifications. For example, PAM will be responsible to activate the databases from a failed server to a healthy one. PAM will be a server in the DAG that owns the cluster quorum resource or the default cluster group. If this server fails, the PAM role is shifted to one of the other servers that takes the ownership of the cluster quorum resource. The SAM role is used to provide information about active database copies to other the components of Exchange, such as Transport services or Client Access services. In the local system, SAM detects the failure of information stores and local databases.

Now, let's take the example of a 4-node DAG that we created earlier in this chapter DAG01 with Exch1, Exch2, Exch3, and Exch4 as members. We are now going to install updates on Exch2, which happens to be acting as a Primary active manager for the DAG01.

In order to prepare Exch2 for maintenance, here are the steps that we will follow:

1. The following command will drain transport queues on Exch2:

    ```
    Set-ServerComponentState Exch2 -Component HubTransport -State
    Draining -Requester Maintenance
    ```

2. You need to restart the transport service to initiate the draining of queues:

    ```
    Restart-Service MSExchangeTransport
    ```

3. This will redirect messages that are yet to be delivered in the local queues to another server, Exch3 in this case:

    ```
    Redirect-Message -Server Exch2 -Target Exch3.contoso.com
    ```

4. The next step is to drain all the Unified Messaging calls from the server called Exch2:

    ```
    Set-ServerComponentState Exch2 -Component UMCallRouter -State
    Draining -Requester Maintenance
    ```

5. As `Exch2` is acting as a PAM, we need to stop `Exch2` to become a PAM by executing the following command:

   ```
   Suspend-ClusterNode Exch2
   ```

6. We now need to move all the active database copies from `Exch2` and prevent them from hosting database copies:

   ```
   Set-MailboxServer Exch2 -DatabaseCopyActivationDisabledAndMoveNow
   $True
   ```

   ```
   Set-MailboxServer Exch2 -DatabaseCopyAutoActivationPolicy Blocked
   ```

7. Finally, the following command will put the server called `Exch2` in the maintenance mode:

   ```
   Set-ServerComponentState Exch2 -Component ServerWideOffline -State
   Inactive -Requester Maintenance
   ```

8. Once the maintenance is complete, we will use the following commands to get the server `Exch2` out of maintenance:

9. The following command will place the server out of the maintenance mode:

   ```
   Set-ServerComponentState Exch2 -Component ServerWideOffline -State
   Active -Requester Maintenance
   ```

10. To start receiving UM calls, do the following:

    ```
    Set-ServerComponentState Exch2 -Component UMCallRouter -State
    Active -Requester Maintenance
    ```

11. The following command will return the server to full cluster functionality:

    ```
    Resume-ClusterNode Exch2
    ```

12. Now, we need the databases to become active and remove activation blocks on `Exch2`:

    ```
    Set-MailboxServer Exch2 -DatabaseCopyActivationDisabledAndMoveNow
    $False
    ```

    ```
    Set-MailboxServer Exch2 -DatabaseCopyAutoActivationPolicy
    Unrestricted
    ```

13. This will enable transport queues on the server:

    ```
    Set-ServerComponentState Exch2 -Component HubTransport -State
    Active -Requester Maintenance
    ```

    ```
    Restart-Service MSExchangeTransport
    ```

14. The following command will display the state of different components on the server if it is ready for the production use:

```
Get-ServerComponentState Exch2 | ft Component,State -Autosize
```

15. If you want to shut down or restart a DAG member, the recommended way is to use the server switchover for moving the active databases to another server using the following command:

```
Move-ActiveMailboxDatabase -Server Exch1
```

Writing a basic script

Here is a simple script that will put a DAG member into maintenance mode and display the result of the component states at the end. We have covered the commands in DAG Maintenance section. The first IF statement will check if the target server is a mailbox server; if it is not, it will exit. I have used the Green Foreground color, but feel free to use a color of your choice based on your Exchange Management shell background. The file name used to save this script is the Start-MaintenanceMode. ps1 file. It takes two mandatory parameters: Server and TargetServerFQDN. Here is an example of putting mailbox server Exch2 in the maintenance mode. Exch3 is another mailbox server, which is part of the same DAG01:

```
<#Start-MaintenanceMode.ps1 -Server Exch2 -TargetServerFQDN Exch3.
contoso.com
#===========
#Parameters
#===========
Param
(
    [Parameter(Mandatory=$true,
            ValueFromPipelineByPropertyName=$true,
            Position=0)]
    [string]$Server=$env:COMPUTERNAME,

    [Parameter(Mandatory=$true,
            ValueFromPipelineByPropertyName=$true,
            Position=1)]
    [string]$TargetServerFQDN
)

#========
#Script
#========
if((Get-ExchangeServer -Identity $TargetServerFQDN | Select
```

```
IsHubTransportServer).IsHubTransportServer -ne $True){
        Write-Host "The target server is not a Mailbox server."
-ForegroundColor Red
            Write-Warning "Aborting script..." -ForegroundColor Red
            Break
    }

   else{
        Write-Host "Draining transport queues on server '$Server' and
restarting Transport on CAS and Mailbox Roles...." -ForegroundColor
Green
        Set-ServerComponentState $Server -Component HubTransport
-State Draining -Requester Maintenance
        Invoke-Command -ComputerName $Server {Restart-Service
MSExchangeTransport -WarningAction SilentlyContinue}
        Invoke-Command -ComputerName $Server {Restart-Service
MSExchangeFrontEndTransport -WarningAction SilentlyContinue}
        Write-Host "Redirecting Messages to '$TargetServerFQDN'..."
-ForegroundColor Green
            Redirect-Message -Server $Server -Target
$TargetServerFQDN -Confirm:$false
        Write-Host "Draining Unified Messaging Calls on server
'$Server'...." -ForegroundColor Green
        Set-ServerComponentState $Server -Component UMCallRouter
-State Draining -Requester Maintenance
        Write-Host "Suspending the cluster node on '$Server'..."
-ForegroundColor Green
    Invoke-Command -ComputerName $Server -ArgumentList $Server
{Suspend-ClusterNode $args[0] | Out-Null}
        Write-Host "Disabling Database Copy Activation and Auto
Activation Policy..." -ForegroundColor Green
        Set-MailboxServer $Server
-DatabaseCopyActivationDisabledAndMoveNow $true
    Set-MailboxServer $Server -DatabaseCopyAutoActivationPolicy
Blocked
        Write-Host "Placing '$Server' in Maintenance mode and
displaying results...." -ForegroundColor Green
        Set-ServerComponentState $Server -Component ServerWideOffline
-State Inactive -Requester Maintenance
        Get-ServerComponentState $Server | ft Component,State
-Autosize

    }
```

The above script is a simple example of how you can automate maintenance using PowerShell. If you would like to add additional logic to your script, review the scripts uploaded by community members at Microsoft TechNet Script Repository.

Here are a couple of examples of scripts used to start and stop the maintenance of Exchange Server 2013:

```
https://gallery.technet.microsoft.com/scriptcenter/Exchange-Server-2013-ff6c942f
```

```
https://gallery.technet.microsoft.com/scriptcenter/Exchange-Server-2013-77a71eb2
```

Summary

In this chapter, we covered high availability and site resilience of mailbox databases in Exchange 2013. You learned the concept of DAG. You also learned using DAG quorum model, managing database copies, and performing maintenance on DAG members.

In the next chapter, you will learn about the use of Exchange Web Services Managed API and how to use it in an Exchange deployment.

Exploring EWS Managed API

Starting with Exchange 2007, **Exchange Web Services** (**EWS**) provides an interface for developers to create custom-client applications that interact with the data stored in an On-Premise or Exchange online mailbox. It allows access to e-mail messages, contacts, calendar, tasks, and public folders that are content programmatically. EWS works by exchanging **Simple Object Access Protocol** (**SOAP**) XML messages for information interchange using HTTP or HTTPS protocols to the Exchange Client Access Servers. In this chapter, we will review the Exchange Web Services application programming interface (API) and its usage in managing an Exchange On-Premise and online organization.

The following topics will be covered in this chapter:

- Introducing Exchange Web Services
- Understanding EWS managed API
- Writing basic EWS managed API code
- Creating custom folders in mailboxes
- Writing a basic script

Introducing Exchange Web Services

With the release of the EWS managed API, you can use it as a wrapper for EWS SOAP calls. It provides an object model, which abstracts complex service descriptions and schema files. It also handles object serialization and deserialization on web requests and responses. It is comparatively easy to use than the autogenerated proxy object models, which do not include autodiscover functionalities and the client-side logic.

You can use the EWS-managed API to access various versions of Exchange 2007 SP1 to Exchange online. Not all the features are available in the EWS managed API. So, you might have to switch to the EWS autogenerated proxy object model if you are looking to use one of the features that are not implemented in the EWS managed API. For example, a folder hierarchy can be created using the EWS Create Folder Path operation in a single call, but this functionality is not available in the EWS managed API.

These are the four primary EWS client development options that you have as a developer. We will focus on the EWS managed API in the rest of the chapter:

- EWS-managed API
- EWS Java API
- EWS autogenerated proxies
- A custom EWS client API

There are three types of applications that can be created using EWS that interacts with Exchange Server or Exchange Online:

- **Client application**: These are independent applications that use EWS to retrieve and write data to the Exchange store. Outlook and Outlook Web App are the examples of client applications.

- **Portal applications**: If you need to use information extracted from Exchange onto a web portal, then you need a portal application. For instance, this is applicable if you would like calendar free/busy information to be published on a SharePoint Web part.

- **Service applications**: These applications use jobs that run in background to synchronize data from Exchange to different systems. If you have a **Customer Relationship Management (CRM)** application and wants your Exchange contacts to be available, you will use a service application.

You can use a common code base for each of these applications. The things that you will change will be the authentication mechanisms. For example, client applications will use user credentials to authenticate using basic or NTLM, whereas service application will use OAuth and impersonation for mailbox access.

Understanding the EWS managed API

Let's take a quick peek into the EWS managed API 2.0 concepts before working on writing a basic client application:

- **Versioning**: Using the EWS managed API, the client needs to set the version when creating an instance of the Exchange Service object. The client can then be made able to access the EWS managed API objects, properties, and methods that are available in this specific version. If the client tries to access an object, property, or method not supported by the version specified, an exception will be thrown.

- **Debugging**: In order to debug applications that are created by the EWS-managed API, we need a combination of tools, such as network monitor tools, built into Visual Studio and internal tools such as network service tracing and logging tools. A part of your code application runs on a server and most of the developers do not have access to. But, you can take a look at the XML requests and responses exchanged between clients and servers to determine the root cause of the issue. The `ExchangeService` object class has the tracking methods that will allow you to capture the XML request sent to Exchange Web Services and the corresponding response returned to the application.

- **Time Zone**: If you are working on a client application using the EWS managed API and would like to interact with items such as Calendar that uses the Date/Time properties, there are certain nuances that you should be aware of. All the date/time strings in EWS are stored in the **Coordinated Universal Time** (**UTC**), which means you don't have to worry about the daylight saving time as it gives an absolute reference for the date/time properties. Unfortunately, this can create confusion for users. So, there are ways in the EWS managed API that allow you to be specific in terms of a time zone when you interact with items that have the Date/Time properties.

- **Item Types**: The strongly typed classes are provided by the EWS managed API that represents a particular item type in the mailbox store such as e-mail messages, post, calendar, or contact items.

- **Security**: The standard security best practices apply to applications developed using the EWS managed API. For example, in order to store passwords of user accounts, the credentials property of the `ExchangeService` object uses the Secure String object to encrypt the password. To manage data confidentiality, the EWS managed API uses secure web connections using the HTTPS protocol. While calling the `AutodiscoverUrl` method on the `ExchangeService` object, if a redirection address is returned that is not a secured (HTTP) session, you can use the `RedirectionUrlValidationCallback` method when you call the `AutodiscoverUrl` method to check the URL and proceed only if the redirection uses HTTPS or the redirection is to a specific group of servers. The server's identity in a EWS call is established by a X509 certificate, and the default self-signed certificate on Exchange servers can be used by setting the `ServerCertificateValidationCallback` property of the `System.Net.ServicePointManager` object. Other security best practices include restricting access to the mailbox owners to connect through EWS or for client applications through application access controls. For example, you can specify a list of client applications to connect or all other applications to connect except the ones that are specifically blocked.

Writing basic EWS managed API code

In order to get started with creating your first EWS managed API application, follow these prerequisites:

- You will need an Exchange On-Premise server or an Exchange online subscription.
- You will need any C# compiler or Visual Studio that supports the .NET framework 4 or later. I am going to show you the steps using Visual Studio 2013. The steps may vary depending on the version of Visual Studio used.
- You will need the EWS managed API 32 or 64 bit depending on your system architecture.

Here are the steps:

1. Launch Visual Studio 2013 and navigate to **File** Menu, **New**, **Project** to launch the **New Project** dialog box

   Use the Visual C# from the **Templates** pane and select **Console Application**.

2. Name the project as `EWSTestEmail` and click on **OK**. This will create the project and open the `Program.cs` code document window.

3. On the **View** Menu, click on the **Open the Solution Explorer** window.

4. Right-click on **References** in the Solution Explorer windows and the
    EWSTestEmail project. Select **Add Reference** in the context menu.
    This will open a dialog box for Reference Manager.

5. Choose **Browse**, and browse to path where the EWS managed API DLL has
    been installed. For example, in my case, I have installed the EWS managed
    API version 2.2, and it is located at C:\Program Files\Microsoft\
    Exchange\Web Services\2.2. Add the file, select the DLL file, and
    click on OK

6. You need to check if the correct version of .NET Framework is used.
    From the Solution Explorer windows right click EWSTestMail project,
    select **properties** and verify that it lists the correct .NET Framework
    version. In my case it lists .NET Framework 4.5.

The next step is to set the ExchangeService object:

1. **Using** keyword is a directive to reference The EWS managed API. Add the
    code to the last using the directive in the Program.cs file:

    ```
    using Microsoft.Exchange.WebServices.Data;
    ```

2. Create an instance of the ExchangeService object with the service version
    depending on your Exchange Environment. For example, the following
    code targets Exchange 2013 SP1 with a variable Exchange 2013:

    ```
    ExchangeService Exchange2013 = new
    ExchangeService(ExchangeVersion.Exchange2013_SP1);
    ```

3. If this is an **On-Premise Exchange Server mailbox** and you are using a
    domain joined client, you can skip this step. Use this if you are using an
    Exchange Online mailbox to pass the username and credentials. For example,
    the following code passes the credentials for Amy Alberts Exchange online
    mailbox:

    ```
    ExchangeOnline.Credentials = new WebCredentials("amya@contoso.
    com", "p@ssw0rd");
    ```

4. If you are using a user account who has a mailbox on Exchange On-Premises,
    which is true in my case as I am using the administrator account, I am going to
    use the following code after we have created an instance of ExchangeService
    class. The default value of UseDefaultCredentials is false, which should be
    set if you are targeting an Exchange online mailbox

    ```
    Exchange2013.UseDefaultCredentials = true;
    ```

5. For the next step, you need to first verify that your Autodiscover service is functioning in your Exchange Organization. Set the AutodiscoverURL method on the instance of the `ExchangeService` object. This will initiate a call to the Autodiscover service to get the URL:

```
Exchange2013.AutodiscoverUrl("administrator@contoso.com");
```

6. Next, we will create an instance of the `EmailMessage` class and pass it to our instance of the `ExchangeService` class:

```
EmailMessage Email = new EmailMessage(Exchange2013);
```

7. Next, we will set the recipient, subject, and body of the message and use the Send method to deliver the message:

```
Email.ToRecipients.Add("administrator@contoso.com");
Email.Subject = "EWSTest Email";
Email.Body = new MessageBody("This is a test email sent by using
the The EWS-managed API");
Email.Send
```

Here is the C# code that you will use in the `Program.cs` file:

```csharp
using System;
using Microsoft.Exchange.WebServices.Data;

namespace EWSTestEmail
{
    class Program
    {
        static void Main(string[] args)
        {
            ExchangeService Exchange2013 = new
ExchangeService(ExchangeVersion.Exchange2013_SP1);

            Exchange2013.UseDefaultCredentials = true;

            Exchange2013.AutodiscoverUrl("administrator@contoso.com");

            EmailMessage Email = new EmailMessage(Exchange2013);

            Email.ToRecipients.Add("administrator@contoso.com");

            Email.Subject = "EWSTest Email";
            Email.Body = new MessageBody("This is a test email sent by
using the The EWS-managed API");
```

```
        Email.Send();


    }
  }
}
```

Creating custom folders in Mailboxes

The following code in the `Program.cs` file will create a folder under the inbox using the `FolderClass` property value of the `IPF.Note`. The folder called `DisplayName` sets the display name as Special Projects. The `folder.save` method will save it under the inbox folder. The rest of the code is used to create the instance of the `ExchangeService` object. It passes the user credentials and sets the `AutodiscoverURL` as discussed in the previous section:

```
using System;
using Microsoft.Exchange.WebServices.Data;

namespace CreateFoldersthroughEWS
{
    class Program
    {
        static void Main(string[] args)
        {
            ExchangeService Exchange2013 = new
ExchangeService(ExchangeVersion.Exchange2013_SP1);

            Exchange2013.UseDefaultCredentials = true;

            Exchange2013.AutodiscoverUrl("administrator@contoso.com");

            // Create a folder called Special Projects under inbox
            Folder folder = new Folder(Exchange2013);
            folder.DisplayName = "Special Projects";
            folder.FolderClass = "IPF.Note";

            // This saves the folder with Inbox as the parent folder.
            folder.Save(WellKnownFolderName.Inbox);

        }
    }
}
```

Writing a basic script

As this book is about managing Exchange using PowerShell, let's use the PowerShell client to save a draft message in the administrator's mailbox. I have installed the EWS managed API 2.2 at `C:\Program Files\Microsoft\Exchange\Web Services\2.2`, which is the default location. You can install it on any other location and ensure that the correct path is referenced.

In my lab, I am using Exchange 2013 Service Pack1, but the process is similar in Exchange 2016 and Exchange online. The only thing that you need to understand is how to target the correct Exchange version that is described next.

The first step is to import the `Microsoft.Exchange.WebServices.dll` module in PowerShell using a variable:

```
$EWSDllPath = "C:\Program Files\Microsoft\Exchange\Web Services\2.2\
Microsoft.Exchange.WebServices.dll"
Import-Module $EWSDllPath
```

The next step is to create the service object just as we did in the earlier sections using C# code in Visual Studio:

```
$Exchange2013 = New-Object Microsoft.Exchange.WebServices.Data.
ExchangeService
```

To look at the properties of the `ExchangeService` instance, you will be able to see the properties as follows:

```
$Exchange2013 | Format-List
```

If you look at the properties of the Service Object `$Exchange2013`, you will see the property `RequestedServerVersion` is set to `Exchange2013_SP1` which is what I have in my lab, so we will move on. If you are using one of the older versions of On-Premise Exchange Servers, you need to set the version using the following format and pass it to the instance of the `ExchangeService` object. For Example, you will use the following code to set the version to Exchange 2010 SP1 and pass it to the `ExchangeService` object:

```
$ExchVersion2010 = [Microsoft.Exchange.WebServices.Data.
ExchangeVersion]::Exchange2010_SP1

$Exchange2010 = New-Object Microsoft.Exchange.WebServices.Data.Exchang
eService($ExchVersion2010)
```

As I am targeting an On-Premise Exchange Server 2013 from a domain-joined client, I will set the value of `UseDefaultCredentials` to `$True` if it is set to `False`:

```
$Exchange2013.UseDefaultCredentials = $True
```

As this is an On-Premise Exchange 2013 installation, I will set the EWS URL on the instance of the `ExchangeService` object as per my On-Premise EWS Virtual directory configuration.

If you are targeting the Exchange online mailbox, the EWS URL should point to `https://outlook.office365.com/EWS/Exchange.asmx`:

```
$Exchange2013.Url = https://mail.contoso.com/EWS/Exchange.asmx
```

Verify that the URL property is set on the object `$Exchange2013` using this:

```
$Exchange2013 | fl
```

Now, we will use the same `EmailMessage` class that we used in the earlier section to create an e-mail message, body, and subject. But, instead of sending the e-mail, we will use the Save method to save the message in the drafts folder:

```
$Email = New-Object Microsoft.Exchange.WebServices.Data.EmailMessage
-ArgumentList $Exchange2013
$Email.Subject = "Test message from EWS using PowerShell"
$Email.From = "administrator@contoso.com"
$Email.ToRecipients.Add("amya@contoso.com")
$Email.Body = "Test from PowerShell client using EWS"
$Email.Save()
```

Here is the Script if you want to run it as a .ps1 file:

```
$EWSDllPath = "C:\Program Files\Microsoft\Exchange\Web Services\2.2\
Microsoft.Exchange.WebServices.dll"
Import-Module $EWSDllPath
$Exchange2013 = New-Object Microsoft.Exchange.WebServices.Data.
ExchangeService
$Exchange2013.UseDefaultCredentials = $True
$Exchange2013.Url = "https://mail.contoso.com/EWS/Exchange.asmx"
$Email = New-Object Microsoft.Exchange.WebServices.Data.EmailMessage
-ArgumentList $Exchange2013
$Email.Subject = "Test message from EWS using PowerShell"
$Email.From = "administrator@contoso.com"
$Email.ToRecipients.Add("amya@contoso.com") | Out-Null
$Email.Body = "Test from PowerShell client using EWS"
$Email.Save()
```

Summary

In this chapter, you learned about using the EWS-managed API to make changes to items in an Exchange On-Premise or Exchange Online Mailbox programmatically. So, if you are a developer and want to know more about the EWS-managed API and things that you can do with this API, review the samples located at `https://code.msdn.microsoft.com/exchange/Exchange-2013-101-Code-3c38582c`.

In the last chapter of this book, we will review some of the common administrative tasks in Exchange and understand how to use PowerShell to save time and effort spent in doing repetitive jobs.

10
Common Administration Tasks

In this chapter, we will use PowerShell cmdlets to perform some of the repetitive tasks that administrators have to do every day.

These are the topics that will be covered in this chapter:

- Managing Active Sync devices
- Managing Databases
- Managing Transport rules and adding disclaimers
- Managing Non-Delivery Reports
- Managing Active Directory Attributes
- Removing old log files
- Health check commands

Managing Active Sync devices

In *Chapter 6, Handling Exchange Server Roles,* you learned how to use Exchange ActiveSync policies and configure mailbox and devices. In this section, we will talk about some of the common challenges that administrators face when it comes to managing ActiveSync devices in their Exchange organization. The first thing that any administrator would like to do is to get a report of all the devices that they have in their organization.

Here is a simple script that will export the devices with their details into a CSV file. The path can be provided as a parameter, or it will use the default c:\temp\log directory:

```
param
(
    [String]$LogPath="C:\temp\log"

)


# Array to collect Device Objects
$Output = @()

# This counter is initialized for the progress bar
$i = 0

# Get a list of ActiveSync Enabled Mailboxes in your Exchange
Organization
$ASMailboxes = Get-CASMailbox -Filter {HasActivesyncDevicePartnership
-eq $true} -ResultSize Unlimited -IgnoreDefaultScope | Where-Object
{$_.ActiveSyncEnabled -eq $true -and $_.DisplayName -notlike "CAS_{*"}

# Loop through Specified Exchange Server ActiveSync Enabled Mailboxes
    ForEach ($ASMailbox in $ASMailboxes)
    {
            # Increase the counter of the progress bar
            $i++

            # Display progress bar
            Write-Progress -Activity "Getting ActiveSync Statistics"
-Status "Exporting for Mailbox $ASMailbox" -PercentComplete (100 *
($i/@($ASMailboxes).count))

            # Get a list of Devices for Each mailbox
            $ASDevices = Get-ActiveSyncDeviceStatistics -Mailbox
$CASMailbox.Identity

            # Loop through each of the Devices
            ForEach ($ASDevice in $ASDevices)
            {
                $Device = New-Deviceect PSObject
                $Device | Add-Member NoteProperty -Name "ServerName"
-Value $ASMailbox.ServerName
                $Device | Add-Member NoteProperty -Name "MailboxName"
-Value $ASMailbox.Name
```

```
                        $Device | Add-Member NoteProperty -Name "DeviceType"
        -Value  $ASDevice.DeviceType
                        $Device | Add-Member NoteProperty -Name "DeviceModel"
        -Value $ASDevice.DeviceModel
                        $Device | Add-Member NoteProperty -Name "DeviceId"
        -Value  $ASDevice.DeviceId
                        $Device | Add-Member NoteProperty -Name "DeviceOS"
        -Value $ASDevice.DeviceOS
                        $Device | Add-Member NoteProperty -Name "DeviceIMEI"
        -Value $ASDevice.DeviceIMEI
                        $Device | Add-Member NoteProperty -Name
        "FirstSyncTime" -Value $ASDevice.FirstSyncTime
                        $Device | Add-Member NoteProperty -Name
        "LastSuccessSync" -Value $ASDevice.LastSuccessSync
                        $Device | Add-Member NoteProperty -Name
        "LastSyncAttemptTime" -Value $ASDevice.LastSyncAttemptTime

                        $Output += $Device
                }
        }

    Write-Progress -Activity "Retrieving ActiveSync Statistics on
    Server $ServerName" -Status "Completed" -Completed

        $Output | Export-Csv -Path "$LogPath\$(get-date -Format "dd-MM-
    yyyy").csv" -Encoding default
```

If you would like to enable or disable certain mailbox services, such as ActiveSync, based on the users Group Membership in Active Directory, you can use the following script. Before using the script, we have created a Security Group called *Exchange ActiveSync Enabled*. Add those users whose ActiveSync needs to be enabled to this group. For the rest, Exchange ActiveSync will be disabled by this script. The script has to run every time there is a change in the Group membership. You can schedule this script to run using Windows Task Scheduler as you have learned in *Chapter 2, Learning Recipient Management*.

Here is the script:

```
# Create an array of all mailboxes in your Exchange Organization
$Mailboxes = Get-Mailbox -ResultSize:unlimited


# Get the users who are member of the group "Exchange ActiveSync Enabled"
$EASUsers = Get-DistributionGroupMember -Identity "Exchange ActiveSync
Enabled"
```

```
# Loop through each item in the Mailboxes array
foreach ($item in $Mailboxes)
{

    # Get the Client Access attributes for the current user
    $Mailbox = Get-CasMailbox -resultsize unlimited -identity $item.Name

    # Check if the User is a member of "Exchange ActiveSync Enabled"
Security Group
    if(($EASUsers | where-object{$_.Name -eq $item.Name}))
    {
        # If the user is enabled for ActiveSync enabled, write it to the
console
        if ($mailbox.ActiveSyncEnabled -eq "true") {Write-Host "Currently
Mailbox for $item is enabled for AciveSync - No change required"}
        # If the user is not enabled for ActiveSync, enable it
        else
        {
            $item | Set-CASMailbox -ActiveSyncEnabled $true
            Write-Host "Enabled ActiveSync for $item"
        }
    }
    # If the user is not a member of "Exchange ActiveSync Enabled" group,
Disable ActiveSync for those users
    else
    {
        if ($mailbox.ActiveSyncEnabled -eq "true")
        {
            $item | Set-CASMailbox -ActiveSyncEnabled $false
            Write-Host "Disabled ActiveSync for $item"
        }
        else
        {
            Write-Host "ActiveSync is already Disabled for $item"
        }
    }
}
```

Managing Databases

Here is a simple script that will display the number and type of mailboxes in the Mailbox Database on the console. For example, if you have five Mailbox Databases in your organization and your user's primary mailbox, the archive mailbox and arbitration mailboxes are distributed across these databases; the script will report these different mailbox types for each mailbox database:

```
$DBs= get-mailboxdatabase | Select Name

$UsersPerDB=@()

get-mailboxdatabase | foreach-object {

        $Object=New-Object PSObject

      $Object | Add-Member NoteProperty -Name "DatabaseName" -Value
$_.name

      $Object | Add-Member NoteProperty -Name "No of User Mailboxes"
-Value (get-mailbox -database $_.name).count

      $Object | Add-Member NoteProperty -Name "No of Archive Mailboxes"
-Value (get-mailbox -database $_.name -Archive).count

      $Object | Add-Member NoteProperty -Name "No of Arbitration
Mailboxes" -Value  (get-mailbox -database $_.name -Arbitration).count

      $UsersPerDB+=$Object

             }


      $UsersPerDB | Format-table –AutoSize
```

As an Exchange Administrator, you need to check the backup of your Exchange Databases. Here is a simple script that will tell you the status of some of the properties of Mailbox Database and will highlight in Red database which are not backed up for 48 hours. You can build on this and include HTML and send a report to a Distribution list as well. You can check the properties that you want to include in your script using this:

```
Get-MailboxDatabase | Get-Member
Here is the script:
$Databases = Get-MailboxDatabase
$TwoDays = (get-date).Addhours(-48)

foreach ($Database in $Databases)

{
        Write-Host "Database Name is  $($Database.Name)"
        Write-Host "BackupInProgress Status is set to $($Database.
BackupInProgress)"
```

```
        Write-Host "SnapshotLastFullBackup is set to $($Database.
SnapshotLastFullBackup)"
        Write-Host "SnapshotLastCopyBackup is set to $($Database.
SnapshotLastCopyBackup)"
        Write-Host "LastFullBackup was taken on $($Database.
LastFullBackup)"
        Write-Host "RetainDeletedItemsUntilBackup is set to
$($Database.RetainDeletedItemsUntilBackup)"

if($Database.LastFullBackup -lt $TwoDays){Write-Host "Alert
BackupFailed for last 2 days" -ForeGroundColor Red}
else {Write-Host "DatabaseBackup is working as expected"
-ForeGroundColor Green}

}
```

Managing Transport rules and adding disclaimers

Transport Rules offer a very granular control to IT admins over the mail flow in your Exchange organization. It can help to build ethical walls between the groups of users; it can protect messages using Active Directory and/or Azure Rights Management Services to encrypt the content and apply disclaimers to messages.

In the first example, we will see how to restrict two groups of users from talking to each other using Exchange Transport Rules. In this case, we will block the e-mail flow between Sales and Research group members except if the message is coming from Peter Houston or Holly Holt who are heading these two groups. You can use multiple conditions (predicates) to build a rule that meets your organization's requirements:

```
New-TransportRule "BlockMessagesBetweenResearchAndSales"
-BetweenMemberOf1 "Sales_SG" -BetweenMemberOf2 "Research_
SG" -ExceptIfFrom "Peter Houston","Holly Holt"
-RejectMessageEnhancedStatusCode "5.7.1" -RejectMessageReasonText "Email
messages sent between the Sales and Research department are blocked as
per IT Policy. Contact your local HelpDesk if you have any questions at
3002"
```

In the second example, we will see how transport rules can be used to automatically protect sensitive content such as employee details, credit card numbers, and more by integrating On-Premise Exchange 2013/2016 or Exchange online with Active Directory or Microsoft Azure Rights management services (RMS). RMS is a technology that works with server and client applications such as Exchange, SharePoint, Office, and more to protect sensitive information by implementing policies to encrypt and control access to the content.

The following command creates a new Transport Protection rule that will automatically apply a RMS template called Do Not Forward to all the messages where the subject line has the word Merger. This will prevent recipients to forward e-mails through the RMS-enabled client application. This needs an existing Active Directory Rights Management Deployment or a subscription to Azure Rights management to work, and you can create templates based on your organization's needs:

```
New-TransportRule -Name "Legal-Mergers" -SubjectContainsWords "Mergers"
-ApplyRightsProtectionTemplate "Do Not Forward"
```

The third and final example of transport rule will be used to create a transport rule to add HTML disclaimers for all the outgoing messaging from the members of All_Contoso_Employees Distribution groups to External Users:

```
New-TransportRule -Name ContosoExternalDisclaimer -SentToScope
'NotInOrganization' -FromMemberOf "All_Contoso_Employees"-
ApplyHtmlDisclaimerText "<h3>Contoso Legal Notice</h3><p>This is
confidential information and if you have received this in error, please
delete this and notify the admin immediately. </p>"
```

Managing Non-Delivery Reports

All the administrators managing Exchange have to deal with Non-Delivery reports. These are automated messages that are sent to senders if Exchange is unable to deliver a message to a recipient or a distribution group. In large Exchange organizations, it is a task for administrators to remove the users who have left the organization from the existing e-mail enabled groups. Here is a simple script that will ask for SamAccountName for the user and remove the group membership of that user account:

Save this file as UserDGCleanup.ps1 and use the following syntax:

```
.\UserDGCleanup.ps1 -SamAccountName <usersamaccountname>
```

Example:

```
.\UserDGCleanup.ps1 -SamAccountName johnd
```

Here is the script

```
param

(
    [Parameter(Mandatory=$true)] [String] $SamAccountName
)
```

```
#Imports the ActiveDirectory Module to execute the AD commandlets

Import-Module -Name ActiveDirectory

# Get the Distinguished name of the user from the Specified SAMAccount
Name

$UserDistinguishedName = Get-ADUser -Properties DistinguishedName
-Identity $SamAccountName

# Get current group memberships for the specified user

$UserGroupMemberships = Get-ADUser -Properties memberof -Identity
$UserDistinguishedName

# Loop through the groups that are mail enabled

    foreach ($GroupDN in $UserGroupMemberships.memberof)

    {

    $Group = Get-ADGroup -Properties mail -Identity $GroupDN

        if($Group.mail -ne "$Null"){Remove-ADGroupMember -Identity
$GroupDN -Members $UserGroupMemberships.DistinguishedName
-Confirm:$false}

    }
```

Managing Active Directory Attributes

Here is a script that will dump disabled users and computer accounts in AD to the
CSV file:

```
Import-Module -Name ActiveDirectory
$DateTime = Get-Date -Format "MM_dd_yyyy_HH_mm"
$FileName = "Disabled_Accounts_$DateTime"
Search-ADAccount -AccountDisabled | Select-Object Name,ObjectClass >>
c:\Scripts\$FileName.csv
```

In the previous script, if you just want to look for disabled user accounts or computers
accounts, change the cmdlet in the last line as follows:

```
Search-ADAccount –AccountDisabled -UsersOnly
Search-ADAccount –AccountDisabled -ComputersOnly
```

The `Search-ADAccount` cmdlet is useful if you want to find out the user's attributes such as expiring passwords, accounts whose passwords are set to never expire, locked out accounts, and so on. Here are some of the examples and, as always, you can use the help of the command using `Get-Help Search-ADAccount`.

If you are reviewing your current Active Directory for security vulnerabilities, one of the things that you would check is accounts, which are set with never-expiring passwords. The following command will retrieve the list of those users:

```
Search-ADAccount -PasswordNeverExpires | Format-Table Name,ObjectClass -
AutoSize
```

If you need the accounts whose passwords have already expired, use the following parameter:

```
Search-ADAccount -PasswordExpired | Format-Table Name,ObjectClass
-AutoSize
```

The following cmdlet will list the accounts that are locked out:

```
Search-ADAccount -LockedOut | Format-Table Name,ObjectClass -AutoSize
```

Based on your requirements, you can use the cmdlet called `Search-ADAccount` to target right users or computer accounts and take action based on your requirements:

There are a few other cmdlets that will help you search users based on their Active Directory attributes. These are `Get-ADUser`, `Get-ADGroup`, `Get-ADComputer`, and `Get-ADObject`.

Here are few examples of these cmdlets.

The following command will list all the groups that are mail-enabled:

```
Get-ADObject -Filter {(mail -like "*") -and (ObjectClass -eq "group")}
```

We can use Get-ADUser or Get-ADObject to find the mail-enabled users as follows:

```
Get-ADUser -Filter {mail -like "*"}
Get-ADObject -Filter {(mail -like "*") -and (ObjectClass -eq "user")}
```

If you are looking to find out universal security groups, type the following:

```
Get-ADGroup -filter {GroupCategory -eq "Security" -and GroupScope -eq
"Universal"}
```

`Get-ADComputer` will list all the computers in your domain. For example:

```
Get-ADComputer -Filter * | Format-Table Name,DistinguishedName -Autosize
```

Removing old log files

Here is a simple script to remove old log files from Exchange Servers at the %ExchangeInstallPath%logging folder. Here, I have used the default installation path of Exchange, but it can be modified to use a variable with a non-default path of the Exchange installation. The number of days can be modified to suit your needs:

```
$Days = 30

$ExchangeLogsPath="C:\Program Files\Microsoft\Exchange Server\V15\
Logging\"

Write-Host "Removing IIS and Exchange logs from Default Directories
except last $Days days"

$Now = Get-Date

$LastModified = $Now.AddDays(-$Days)

$LogFiles = Get-ChildItem $ExchangeLogsPath -Include *.log -Recurse |
Where {$_.LastWriteTime -le "$LastModified"}

foreach ($File in $LogFiles)

{Write-Host "Deleting file $File" -ForegroundColor Red; Remove-Item
$File -ErrorAction SilentlyContinue | out-null}
```

Health check commands

Exchange Server 2013 and 2016 provide test cmdlets to test a lot of different scenarios. In order to get a list of the test cmdlets available, use the following command. I have used the Where-Object filter to filter out the test cmdlets from other modules:

```
Get-Command -Verb Test | where-object module -match Exchange01.contoso.
com
```

Here, we will cover some of the health check cmdlets available with Exchange 2013 and 2016. The first step is to create a test user mailbox, which is required by some of these test cmdlets. The script provided for this purpose and is called new-TestCasConnectivityUser.ps1; it is located in %ExchangeInstallPath%Scripts folder. Once executed with no parameters, it will prompt you for a password for the test account and create the user.

Test-ActiveSyncConnectivity

Now, let's test the ActiveSync connectivity on the client access server Exchange01. For this, we will use the Test-ActiveSyncConnectivity cmdlet, which simulates an ActiveSync connection from a mobile device to a mailbox:

```
Test-ActiveSyncConnectivity -ClientAccessServer Exchange01
```

Say you are troubleshooting ActiveSync for a user, John Doe, type this:

```
Test-ActiveSyncConnectivity -MailboxCredentials (Get-Credential johnd@
contoso.com)
```

Test-ReplicationHealth

This cmdlet is used to check the status of Replication and log replay for mailbox servers, which are a part of a Database Availability Group. This checks different components such as Active Manager, network components, cluster service, and quorum resources. You can run this cmdlet against both local and remote DAG members.

If you want to test the replication health of mailbox server Exchange01, type this:

```
Test-ReplicationHealth -Identity Exchange01
```

Test-OutlookWebServices

This cmdlet is used to verify scenarios such as Autodiscover, Exchange Web Services, Availability Service, and Offline Address Book for Microsoft Outlook.

Here is a command to test whether the preceding services are working for a specific mailbox:

```
Test-OutlookWebServices -Identity:amya@contoso.com -MailboxCredential
(Get-Credential amya@contoso.com)
```

Get-Server Health

If you are looking to check the health of your Exchange 2013 servers, use the Get-ServerHealth cmdlet:

```
Get-ServerHealth -Identity Exchange01
```

This will return a lot of useful information, such as HealthSet Names, Alert Values, and Server components.

Summary

In this chapter, we covered some common administrative tasks that can be performed using simple PowerShell scripts. As with most of the chapters in this book, we tried to keep the scripts simple to understand and reuse. Once you have a basic idea of how scripting works in PowerShell, you can work on advance scripting techniques such as using functions that can be reused in a script.

Index

V

values
  retrieving, from array 18, 19
variables
  $_ 9
  $Error 9
  $Home 9
  $NULL 9
  assignment operators 9-11
  comparison operators 11, 12
  using 8, 9
versioning 161

W

While loops 16
Windows PowerShell
  about 2, 3
  basic script, writing 25
  benefits 3
  help system 6
  syntax 4-6
  versions 4
**Windows Public Key Infrastructure
    certificates 79**

Thank you for buying
Microsoft Exchange Server PowerShell Essentials

About Packt Publishing

Packt, pronounced 'packed', published its first book, *Mastering phpMyAdmin for Effective MySQL Management*, in April 2004, and subsequently continued to specialize in publishing highly focused books on specific technologies and solutions.

Our books and publications share the experiences of your fellow IT professionals in adapting and customizing today's systems, applications, and frameworks. Our solution-based books give you the knowledge and power to customize the software and technologies you're using to get the job done. Packt books are more specific and less general than the IT books you have seen in the past. Our unique business model allows us to bring you more focused information, giving you more of what you need to know, and less of what you don't.

Packt is a modern yet unique publishing company that focuses on producing quality, cutting-edge books for communities of developers, administrators, and newbies alike. For more information, please visit our website at www.packtpub.com.

About Packt Enterprise

In 2010, Packt launched two new brands, Packt Enterprise and Packt Open Source, in order to continue its focus on specialization. This book is part of the Packt Enterprise brand, home to books published on enterprise software – software created by major vendors, including (but not limited to) IBM, Microsoft, and Oracle, often for use in other corporations. Its titles will offer information relevant to a range of users of this software, including administrators, developers, architects, and end users.

Writing for Packt

We welcome all inquiries from people who are interested in authoring. Book proposals should be sent to author@packtpub.com. If your book idea is still at an early stage and you would like to discuss it first before writing a formal book proposal, then please contact us; one of our commissioning editors will get in touch with you.

We're not just looking for published authors; if you have strong technical skills but no writing experience, our experienced editors can help you develop a writing career, or simply get some additional reward for your expertise.

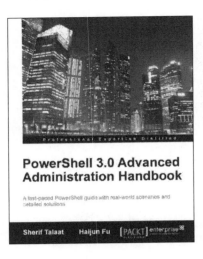

PowerShell 3.0 Advanced Administration Handbook

ISBN: 978-1-84968-642-6   Paperback: 370 pages

A fast-paced PowerShell guide with real-world scenarios and detailed solutions

1. Discover and understand the concept of Windows PowerShell 3.0.

2. Learn and gain the advanced topics and techniques for a professional PowerShell scripting.

3. Explore the secret of building custom PowerShell snap-ins and modules.

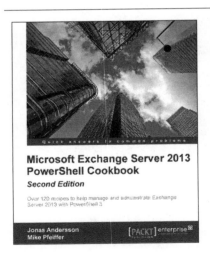

Microsoft Exchange Server 2013 PowerShell Cookbook

Second Edition

ISBN: 978-1-84968-942-7   Paperback: 504 pages

Over 120 recipes to help manage and administrate Exchange Server 2013 with PowerShell 3

1. Newly updated and improved for Exchange Server 2013 and PowerShell 3.

2. Learn how to write scripts and functions, schedule scripts to run automatically, and generate complex reports with PowerShell.

3. Manage and automate every element of Exchange Server 2013 with PowerShell such as Mailboxes, distribution groups and Address lists.

Please check **www.PacktPub.com** for information on our titles

Windows PowerShell 4.0
for .NET Developers

ISBN: 978-1-84968-876-5   Paperback: 140 pages

A fast-paced PowerShell guide, enabling you
to efficiently administer and maintain your
development environment

1. Enables developers to start adopting Windows
   PowerShell in their own application to extend
   its capabilities and manageability.

2. Introduces beginners to the basics, progressing
   on to advanced level topics and techniques
   for professional PowerShell scripting and
   programming.

3. Step-by-step guide, packed with real world
   scripts examples, screenshots, and best
   practices.

Windows PowerShell for .NET
Developers

Second Edition

ISBN: 978-1-78528-743-5   Paperback: 330 pages

Efficiently administer and maintain your development
environment with Windows PowerShell

1. Explore scripting and automation techniques
   with Windows PowerShell.

2. Gain concrete knowledge of Windows
   PowerShell scripting to perform professional
   level scripting.

3. Discover the benefits of the Configuration
   Management Platform with this step-by-
   step guide that includes real-world scripting
   examples.

Please check **www.PacktPub.com** for information on our titles

Made in the USA
Middletown, DE
18 August 2016